1 IN 10 SURVIVOR

LIFE AFTER CARDIAC ARREST

ALAN OWEN

Copyright © 2022 Alan Owen

All rights reserved. No part of this book may be used or reproduced by any means, graphic, electronic, or mechanical, including photocopying, recording, taping or by any information storage retrieval system without the written permission of the author except in the case of brief quotations embodied in critical articles and reviews.

ISBN: 9798370675713

Because of the dynamic nature of the Internet, any web addresses or links contained in this book may have changed since publication and may no longer be valid. The views expressed in this work are solely those of the author and do not necessarily reflect the views of the publisher, and the publisher hereby disclaims any responsibility for them.

The author of this book does not dispense financial or medical advice or prescribe the use of any technique without the advice of a physician or financial advisor. The intent of the author is only to offer information of a general nature. In the event you use any of the information in this book for yourself, which is your constitutional right, the author and the publisher assume no responsibility for your actions.

British Cataloguing Publication Data: A catalogue record of this book is available from The British Library.

Also available on Kindle.

CONTENTS

Introduction 5

About Me and My Family 7

D-Day 10

D-Day (Mel's Point of View) 18

D-Day (Amanda's Point of View) 23

Hospitalisation 27

Back Home: A Time of Reflection 37

Heart Attack vs Cardiac Arrest 40

Living with an ICD 44

Medication 48

Driving & DVLA 51

Reaching Out 55

Finances 58

Life Insurance 61

UK Benefits 67

Visiting the Team 72

Returning to the Football Tournament 75

Defibrillator and CPR 77

Visiting the Air Ambulance 81

Visiting Caldicot Leisure Centre 87

Meeting the PM 90
Coming to Terms Mentally and Physically 95
Online Support 101
Understanding Cardiomyopathy 104
Genetics 108
Helping Raise Awareness 110
Making a Will 113
Work 116
Day to Day 120
Living Differently 123
Advice 126
Addendum 134

INTRODUCTION

This book is dedicated to everyone who has suffered an out-of-hospital Sudden Cardiac Arrest (SCA) or has been involved in one at some point in their life. If you have, and you are reading this, then your life has changed forever; it will never be the same. For those of us who survived, our odds (according to the British Heart Foundation) are 1 in 10. The 10 percenters. For those who are not so lucky (I will use this word a lot through this book), the loss is incredibly significant. A sudden death of any sort has a major impact on the lives of those we leave behind.

I am lucky to be here, writing this book. I was in the right place to have my SCA, near the best facilities, and I am forever grateful to those people who saved me: friends, the staff at Caldicot Leisure Centre, the Wales Air Ambulance, and the staff at the Heath Hospital in Cardiff. It is because of these people that I can sit here and write this book. If I was on my own during my SCA, I would have died, there is no doubt.

This book will show the highs and lows of my journey from SCA through the period of the first eight months of my recovery. It has been a rollercoaster ride for my whole family, but especially for my wife Mel and my son Joseph, who are with me every day and ensure I keep my feet on the ground and do not rush back.

To Martin, who put me in the recovery position, and Sean, who performed CPR; to Justin, Kirsty and Briden (the staff at the leisure centre) and the medical professionals who took over my care: thank you does not seem enough. There are no words I can say or actions I can perform to express my gratitude. I now have a second chance and I intend to take it.

ABOUT ME AND MY FAMILY

My name is Alan Owen, and I live in a small village in Carmarthenshire called Llanddarog, in a house named Lletty-Dau-Filwr. For the non-Welsh speakers, we too struggled to pronounce the name when we bought the house in 2017. It translates as 'Two Soldiers Accommodation', as two soldiers were rescued from a plane crash and looked after in the house during World War II.

At the time of my SCA I was 51; I was fit and healthy and had no symptoms. I had recently joined Carmarthen Town walking football team and was playing regularly.

I live with my wife Mel and my son Joseph, who was 15 years old at the time of my SCA. Joseph had been diagnosed with epilepsy in 2018, but, with medication, had been seizure-free for nearly a year.

I owned two companies, ICARIS Ltd and ICARIS Sentinel Ltd, and both were doing well. We had survived the COVID pandemic and adopted a work-from-home model for the staff. I had also co-founded a Charitable Incorporated Company, LABRATS

(Legacy of the Atomic Bomb. Recognition for Atomic Test Survivors), which was campaigning for recognition in the UK for the British nuclear test veterans and their families. I became involved because my father was present on Christmas Island for 24 detonations in 78 days during Operation Dominic in 1962.

We were running the #lookmeintheeye campaign in conjunction with the Daily Mirror and Susie Boniface, who has campaigned tirelessly for over 20 years. We had made progress and met with Sir Keir Starmer, who backed the campaign. We had also met with Andy Burnham and Steve Rotheram and joined the #HillsboroughLawNow campaign.

Life was good. It was very busy, but we were financially stable and living with two border collies and a working cocker spaniel, Oreo, Monty and Arthur, on a 100-acre farm (we did not own the land, just the farmhouse.) We were helping many veterans and educating the world about nuclear testing and the effects on the servicemen and the planet.

Our family history is not good. My father, James Ronald Owen, died in 1994 from a heart attack (which I now know is different to a cardiac arrest) at the age of 52. In 1996, my brother Gordon also died from a heart attack; it was incredibly hard to deal with, as he was only 31 years old. My mother (who died in 2011) never recovered from losing her husband and oldest son within 18 months of each other. My sister was born blind in her left eye and has also suffered a heart attack.

We were fully aware of the issues within the family, and I underwent tests in 1997, though no problems were reported at the time.

Football and fast cars have always been my passion. Joseph played for a local football team, Pwll Athletic, and I had officiated a number of their games during their 2021-2022 season and enjoyed the run out and interacting with the boys. In December 2021, I played in a full charity match for Joseph's team and enjoyed it so much that I joined the walking football team. I was enjoying kicking a football again, albeit at a slower pace, after many years of not playing; it was fantastic fun and great exercise.

Little did I know, at the beginning of April 2022, that my world was about to be turned upside down.

D-DAY

Walking football was going well, both training and playing friendly matches. It was a different style of football than I was used to. I would describe it as a 6-a-side game which, for 10-12 minutes, is very intense. You must be mentally switched on, have very accurate passing, and keep moving to make space. It is a very good workout, and I would recommend it to anyone over 50 who has played football and wants to get back into the sport.

We were due to play our first league games in a tournament at Caldicot Leisure Centre on 3rd April 2022. The day started out fine. I woke Joseph, who was coming to watch the tournament, and we ate breakfast. Then I prepared my kit bag, kissed my wife goodbye, told her "See you later," and we drove the hour and a half to the leisure centre.

We changed into our kit in the changing rooms, and I laughed and joked with the lads as we prepared for our first match.

This is where my memory ends. I have no recollection of the match, my SCA, or the next few days in hospital; it is a complete blank. I now know that it is not unusual not to remember a sudden cardiac arrest and that many people have no recollection of the incident, of minutes or hours beforehand and for days afterwards. I still do not remember what happened, so I am relying on the memories of friends, my wife, my sister, and the air ambulance report.

We played the first match, and we were waiting for the next match to start, watching our 'A' team play another game. I was talking to Martin when, according to him, I just collapsed mid-sentence. I hit the floor and he immediately put me in the recovery position. He checked my pulse, and it was initially faint. Then nothing. Martin is an ex-police officer and trained in such incidents, so he knew I was in trouble.

Sean (who is ex-military) saw me collapse and stopped playing. He ran over to me and immediately started CPR. Our manager, Josh, called 999, and then asked if there was a defibrillator available at the leisure centre. Luckily for me, the centre had one, and it was with me in minutes.

For anyone reading this who has never had any defibrillator training, the new machines talk you through the process of administering a shock and if the heart is not able to receive a shock, it will not administer one. Luckily for me, my heart had gone into VF (ventricular fibrillation) before stopping and after Kirsty administered three shocks, my heart started beating again. Justin and Briden from the leisure centre performed further rounds of CPR and

Justin gave me mouth to mouth.

Ventricular fibrillation (VF) is a fast and chaotic heart rhythm that occurs in the lower chambers, or ventricles. In VF, the heart loses its ability to pump effectively. This results in a drop of blood pressure and loss of consciousness and then the heart can stop beating (as in my case). If normal rhythm is not restored, it will result in death.

My teammates and the leisure centre staff were incredible, and I was lucky that I had experienced people around me who had been trained to administer CPR and in the use of a defibrillator. I would encourage everyone to undertake both CPR and defibrillator training so they are prepared in case of an emergency.

The 999 call was received at 10:52 and the call centre decided to scramble the Wales Air Ambulance to the scene to enable a quick response. With the football tournament now cancelled, the other players removed the goals and nets so the air ambulance could land. Within just 20 minutes of me collapsing, the paramedics were at my side. My condition was assessed and it was decided that I needed a general anaesthetic and a ventilator to assist me with breathing, as I was agitated.

I now know that the Glasgow Coma Scale (GCS) was used to assess me when the air ambulance crew arrived. For anyone not familiar with this scale, it is used to describe the level of consciousness in a person following trauma. The GCS is a reliable and objective way of recording the initial and subsequent levels of consciousness in a person after a brain injury. It is used by trained staff at the site of an event like a car crash or sports injury, for example, and in the emergency department and intensive care units.

A GCS of 8 or less is classed as severe. When the crew arrived and I was assessed (this was after the defibrillator was used), I was scored as a 4. The scale runs from 0 to 15. I was in serious trouble.

Unfortunately, the air ambulance crew that attended did not include a doctor who could administer the anaesthetic, so another helicopter was sent to the scene with a doctor on board. The response team had effectively set up an emergency room on the football pitch around me and were ensuring I did not suffer another cardiac arrest.

I was given the anaesthetic and put on a ventilator. It was decided that I needed to be transferred by road ambulance to Heath Hospital in Cardiff. This was because there was no room in the helicopter to perform CPR and my condition was such that I could have another arrest en route. If this was to happen in a road ambulance, they could stop and administer CPR.

My main regret of the day is that Joseph saw the entire incident. He was taking penalties on a spare pitch when it happened; he saw the CPR and knew I was in a bad way. Again, members of the football team were amazing. They took him to one side and then into the main building whilst the medical team worked on me. They asked Joseph about our family history, and he was brave enough to tell them about his grandfather, uncle and aunt and their heart attacks.

Mike from the football team called Mel to tell her what had happened. This is a phone call that no one wants to make. I was still in the hands of the medics and, in the words of Ruby, who was the first member of the medical team to see me, I was very poorly.

Mel dropped a key in to the neighbours, asked them to look after the dogs and immediately drove towards Caldicot, as she didn't know where I was being taken or my condition. She tells me that she was fit to drive, and she was OK, but it must have been a terrible time, not knowing if I was going to survive.

She called my sister Laura from the car and told her about the incident, and my sister immediately made plans to travel to Wales from Cheltenham to provide support. Mel also telephoned a friend, Amanda, who lives in Chepstow. She explained the situation and asked if Amanda could look after Joseph, who was still at the leisure centre.

Amanda arrived while I was receiving treatment. She ensured Joseph was OK and kept Mel informed about where the ambulance was taking me. She kept Mel calm and told her that I was OK, I was alive and responding to treatment.

Mel diverted to Heath Hospital, Amanda took Joseph to the hospital, and I was transported unconscious on a ventilator to the hospital by road ambulance. Mel was already at the hospital when they brought me in, with Amanda, Joseph and my sister arriving shortly afterwards.

I then underwent several tests, including a brain scan to see if I had any blood clots or had suffered any damage to my brain. Approximately four hours later, Mel, Joseph and my sister Laura were allowed to see me. I had been taken off the ventilator but was still very drowsy. They tell me I was sick when they entered the room, but I was communicating with them.

I don't remember any of this. My brain has blanked it out. It could be because of the drugs or, as it has been explained to me, the trauma I suffered.

At one point, the nurses asked me if I knew who Mel was and I replied "No." They asked me if I knew my sister and I also replied "No." About an hour later, they asked me the same questions and I replied that I knew them – and, apparently, I replied like it was a stupid question. A good sign that I had not suffered any significant brain damage.

My ex-wife, Joseph's mother Jenny picked up Joseph and returned to the house to look after the dogs, whilst Mel and Laura remained at the hospital.

For 27.5 hours they waited, sitting on plastic chairs and eating biscuits, to make sure I was OK. At one point, Ruby came past the door of the room in resus where I was, as she had travelled with another patient to the hospital. She walked past, stopped, and then came back and said to Mel: "What is he doing?" as I was sitting up with no oxygen or ventilation. She could not believe I was awake and communicating, as my condition on the football pitch had been extremely serious.

I was then transferred from resus to a cardiac care ward to begin a new chapter of my life, one which I almost didn't have. Without the help of my friends, the leisure centre staff, the air ambulance and the NHS staff, I would not have made it. If I had been walking the dogs on my own, or driving my car on my own, I would be dead. It is a very sobering thought and one that is difficult to get your head around.

I have experienced death. I saw my father's body minutes after he died, and I watched my mother pass away from cancer in a nursing home. I have seen my brother, uncle and cousins in funeral parlours. We all die; it is the one thing we can be guaranteed of. Life changes in an instant, but it was not my time to go. Mel told me that she looked at a picture of my dad and uncle (both of whom have passed) and said: "You can't have him. Not yet," before she left that day.

I do not know why my SCA happened at that time at that location, but it did. Some will call it fate; others will say that someone is looking over me. My nurse called it a 'perfect storm'. All I know is that, without some very brave and professional people, I would not be here today.

D-DAY
(MEL'S POINT OF VIEW)

The morning of 3rd April 2022 started like any other. Our oldest dog is our early morning alarm clock, as she barks at 6am. My turn to get up and see to the dogs that morning.

Not long after I had fed the dogs, I heard footsteps as Alan got up and woke Joseph so they could start to get ready to leave for Caldicot.

After the usual morning rush, breakfast and kiss goodbye, "I love you, see you later," I got ready for a morning of coffee and TV.

Around 10.45, I decided it was time to get dressed and get on with my day. This thought was disturbed by my mobile phone ringing in my dressing gown pocket. Seeing Joseph's name appear on the screen, I answered it. This phone call would change my life.

A voice that was not Joseph's asked if he was speaking to Mel. "Yes," I said. The gentleman told me his name was Mike Stacy and he was one of the walking football team. He told me Alan had collapsed at the football tournament. My initial thought was that he hadn't eaten enough that morning, but this thought soon disappeared.

Mike told me, very calmly, that Alan was receiving CPR, the defib machine was on its way and Josh was on the phone to the ambulance service.

I shot bolt upright out of the chair and started to pace around the kitchen. I had to ask him to repeat what he had said. I think my words were: "Did you just say CPR?"

He repeated himself and I immediately asked where Joseph was, and how he was. I briefly spoke to Joseph and told him not to worry and that I would send someone to get him.

The Leisure Centre is over an hour from our house, so I called my friend Amanda, who lives in Chepstow, about eight miles from Caldicot. To this day I am not sure how I managed to think straight. I went into a sort of survival mode. Amanda did not answer the phone, so I texted her and then video-called her. Finally, she answered. She took one look at my face and said: "What the f**k has happened?"

I could not form sentences and just kept repeating, "Alan… CPR… Defib… Joseph… Caldicot. Help me!" Finally, I took a deep breath and asked her to get in her car and drive to Caldicot Leisure Centre to collect Joseph and see how Alan was. Amanda was off like a rocket.

Joseph now sorted, I needed to get dressed. I ran from room to room like a headless chicken, not able to breathe properly and shouting, "Not yet!" and "Oh my god." There's a picture hanging above my chest of drawers of Alan's dad and uncle, now both deceased, and I pointed to them and said: "You can't have him – not yet."

Once dressed (in God knows what), I locked the dogs away, gave the house key to our neighbour, explained the situation and sped off in my car.

The next thing I had to do was ring Alan's sister. This was the hardest phone call to make. I was in the car, calling hands-free, and Laura answered straight away – she never answers straight away! Without even saying hello, I said I had something to tell her and told her not to panic. "Alan's collapsed playing football. He needed CPR and a shock from a defibrillator," I told her. "I'm in the car heading up the M4 but I don't know which hospital I'm heading to."

To this day, the sound of her voice on that call still haunts me. "I'm coming," she said. "Drive carefully."

Somewhere along the M4 (at 90mph), Amanda called me. She had got to Joseph and seen Alan. She lied and told me he looked fine and that he was going by air ambulance to Cardiff Vale Hospital. I said I would see her there. Then I called Laura and told her which hospital to head for. She asked how he was, and I said he had been put on a ventilator to help him breathe.

Cardiff Vale is a massive hospital with nine different carparks. I screeched into a parking space and ran down an access ramp to an exit door. A car came up the ramp and just as I was about to shout at the driver, I realised it was Amanda and Joseph. It still amazes me to this day that we ended up in the same car park. She parked next to me and we headed to the A&E department.

There was a queue and I pushed my way to the front. I am not usually a confident person, but no one was getting in my way that day. "You have to help me!" I said. "My husband is being rushed here by air ambulance." No one in the queue complained that we had pushed to the front once they heard that.

The team took us straight to a relatives' room to wait. When Laura arrived, I went to meet her and brought her to the room. On reflection, the fact that we were ushered into the relatives' room showed how serious the situation was, but I failed to realise that at the time.

We waited in that room for four hours, not knowing if Alan was dead or alive. Finally, a consultant came in. "Alan's had lots of tests and scans," he said. "They show no blood clots and no sign of a stroke but he has suffered a Sudden Cardiac Arrest. He is just being taken off the ventilator and then you can see him."

When I first saw Alan, he was not a man I recognised. He was pale and grey and he looked so small and frightened as he lay in the bed. He spent 27 ½ hrs in that resus bed before he was moved into CCU. I sat there for 27 ½ hrs watching his heart monitor, not wanting or able to fall asleep, frightened that the man I love – my world, my rock, my everything – would be taken away from me.

D-DAY
(AMANDA'S POINT OF VIEW)

Normal start to the day: red wine hangover and Facetiming Susan to complain about said hangover. Mel was ringing and I tell Susan that's unusual, but I'll call her later. Two minutes later, Mel is Facetiming me so I tell Susan I will call her back as it must be important.

Mel's distraught face appears. "Please help me!"

"What the fuck has happened?!"

She whimpers through a series of words: "Alan... football... collapse... CPR." Then she says, "Joseph is there on his own."

You know when someone says they are instantly sober? Well, this is one of those moments. I just stare at her, confused. "I don't know what you are saying to me," I say. My brain refuses to accept it. "I'll go and get Joseph and I'll call you back. Where are they again?"

"Caldicot Leisure Centre."

"Right. I am on my way, Mel. I'll get Joseph."

I'm in the car, begging a god I don't believe in to make sure everything is okay. Still piecing together what Mel had said, I turn into the leisure centre car park and see the air ambulance. I'm off… I just run towards the people in the hi-vis jackets. As I approach, I see a man on a stretcher. *OMG, that's Alan. Deep breath, Amanda. Stay fucking calm. No one needs you having a panic attack on top of this. Detach, stay strong, do your job.* I speak to the first medic I see. "Where is Joseph?" He tells me he's with the staff inside and I am off again, barrelling through people. Bursting through the door, I see a lady at reception and just say: "Joseph?"

"He's in here with us."

I go in. He's wearing your coat and I just give him the biggest hug. "Are you okay?" I ask him, for the first of about a thousand times. I call Mel to let her know I have Joseph with me and that he's okay. "I'll get more info on what's happening." Mel tells me she's driving but doesn't know where she is heading. "I'll find out," I say. *Next job, Amanda: find out which hospital they are going to.*

The man staying with Joseph is watching the pitch on a security camera. He briefs me on events so far. You collapsed, they administered CPR and defib, your heart was beating again, and the air ambulance are working to get you stable enough to fly. I watch with him. They start wheeling you towards the helicopter, but they stop and wheel you back out again. *What's going on?* I turn to Joseph. "I'm going to find out what's happening. I'll be back." Joseph wants to come too.

We walk down to the pitch. You are surrounded by equipment and medics; it doesn't look good. Joseph and I are greeted by a lady in red – I find out later this was Ruby. She explains to us that there is another air ambulance with a doctor who can administer the medication you need to send you to sleep so you can be safely transported. I think I know what she means: they are going to put you on a ventilator. I turn to look at you on the stretcher. Your skin is grey and your body is jerking off the bed as you fight for your life, while medics are supporting your airway and forcing oxygen into your lungs. *Fuck, fuck, fuck.* Yor body calms and you are still. I check your chest – up, down, up, down. You are breathing – not especially well, but still breathing.

Ruby asks if we want to talk to you before we leave; she says you can still hear us. Joseph walks over to you and places his hand on your shoulder. "Come on, Dad. You'll be alright, mate. I'll see you soon." At this point I realise Joseph doesn't understand what he is seeing. I have to call Mel, with Joseph next to me, and I have to make a decision: tell Mel the truth, let Joseph hear the truth and have both of them panic, or lie to Mel, get her safely to the hospital and keep Joseph calm. I know stress can trigger a seizure. I call Mel, tell her you are breathing and just waiting on a doctor to arrive so they can transport you safely to Cardiff Vale Hospital. I tell her all will be okay; you will be fine. I might be wrong, but it was a risk I had to take; I didn't know any more than she did. *I'm sorry I lied, Mel.*

Joseph and I leave for the hospital just as the second air ambulance lands. On the journey I am talking nonsense to Joseph about his car plans and other things, keeping to the speed limit, trying not to panic him. Everything is fine. *EVERYTHING IS NOT FINE, AMANDA!* Amazingly, we find the multistorey car park and Mel. I hug her tight and we all go to A&E. Standing outside, waiting for someone to come and take us in, I'm holding her hand for comfort and reassurance. "When I saw Alan last, it was like an operating theatre on the pitch," I tell her. "So that's good."

"That is not good, Amanda," Mel says.

You had everything you needed to save you, I think. *That is… good? I look at Mel and Joseph. If you die, how am I going to get them through this?*

We are taken to the relatives' room and the waiting begins. Mel turns to me and says, "I can't lose him, not now. What if I lose him?"

I hug her. "You're not going to lose him," I say. My heart is broken for her. All I can think is, *Alan, if you can magically still hear me then fight harder. Please don't leave her.*

HOSPITALISATION

I was admitted to CCU (a critical cardiac care ward) where I could be monitored before being transferred to a normal ward. My consultant was Professor Yousef and he decided, based on my results, that I needed two stents fitted because of a blockage that was restricting the blood flow. The blockage didn't cause the cardiac arrest but, having been picked up on the CT scan, it required surgery, which was arranged for the next day. My memory of that time is still not good.

I remember being told I needed to have the stents, but do not remember the actual procedure, apart from waking up afterwards with a plastic sleeve on my wrist.

The procedure is called an angioplasty, and it involves inserting a short wire-mesh tube, called a stent, into the artery. The stent is left in place permanently to allow blood to flow more freely. The procedure is commonplace and involves the stent being inserted via a catheter in an artery. When the catheter is in place, a thin wire is guided down the length of the coronary artery using X-ray video, delivering a small balloon to the affected section. This is then inflated to widen the artery, squashing fatty deposits against the artery wall so blood can flow through more freely when the deflated balloon is removed. The stent is placed around the balloon before it's inserted and it expands when the balloon is inflated and remains in place when the balloon is deflated and removed.

I was not aware at the time how the stents would be inserted. I assumed they would enter via my groin, as I had seen this type of procedure on TV, but I was mistaken. The entry location is in the right wrist; they feed the stent through your arm, across your chest and into place, alleviating the blockage and minimising the need for any major incisions or surgery.

I had two stents fitted; I have since spoken to someone who had six, but the procedure is the same. I am no medical expert, but I felt better after researching the surgery; other people may not want to know, but I did. I've since joined several online forums and I now know that everyone is different. We've had different procedures, different diagnoses, but we have one thing in common and that is we have suffered a sudden cardiac arrest, which is different to a heart attack. A cardiac arrest is when the heart malfunctions and stops beating unexpectedly; a heart attack is due to blood flow to the heart being stopped.

When I returned from the procedure, I noticed I had a plastic cuff on my right arm. This cuff, which was covering the entry point in my wrist, was under pressure. Every hour, the pressure was reduced by the nurses until the cuff was removed. All I was left with was a small insertion point. It is an incredible procedure, considering the impact it has on increasing the blood flow, yet there was little or no evidence to show it had been performed. The skills of the medical team are incredible.

For anyone who has to have a stent fitted, I did not feel them at all. Some people I have spoken to have experienced chest pain and problems, but I have had no pain, no issues and do not feel them. I am now left with nothing to show the procedure ever happened. Modern medicine is incredible, and I felt the difference immediately.

~

Whilst recovering in hospital, I wore a portable heart monitor and was monitored 24/7. My vital signs were consistent and I had no issues. The monitor was problematic to wear, and showering involved putting the monitor in a plastic glove which was taped shut, but it was very reassuring to know that my signs were good.

I was sitting up in my hospital bed, three days after dying, recovering from a stent operation. It had been an unbelievable few days. So much had happened and I was trying to comprehend the seriousness of it all. My memory of those days has still not returned but my wife tells me many stories about how I was sick, didn't recognise her and kept asking her what had happened. I do not remember any of it.

I was not worried about the things I had worried about before, such as work and bills etc. Nothing was as important as reflecting on the fact that I had survived. I was told to rest and take it easy, which I did. You quickly get used to the hospital routine: breakfast, lunch and dinner, with tests and doctor visits in between. Each day merges into the next and you soon forget what day it is.

Like many of us, I do not like being in hospital. They are fantastic places but I did not want to be in any longer than was necessary. I just wanted to go home. Thinking back to that time, the seriousness of my situation had not sunk in. What my body had gone through, the trauma – both physically and mentally – was yet to become apparent.

However, I felt better almost instantly; the two stents were already providing increased blood flow. I hoped this would be the last surgical procedure, but I was wrong.

The nurse told me I had suffered six broken ribs during the CPR, which is common, and these would become more and more painful. Sean and the staff at Caldicot Leisure Centre had done an amazing job of administering CPR, keeping the oxygen flowing to my brain and ensuring I did not suffer any major brain damage. For this, my family and I are eternally grateful; no words can express my gratitude.

I was also told I had been diagnosed with

hypertrophic cardiomyopathy, or HCM, which is a condition where the muscles of the heart thicken over time, preventing the heart from pumping blood correctly. It can be genetic and I would need to undergo genetic testing. If it was found that I had the gene, my son would also need to be tested and so would my sister. This came as a shock to us all as, to my knowledge, no one in my family had ever been diagnosed with any form of cardiomyopathy.

It was recommended that I have an ICD fitted because of my SCA and cardiomyopathy diagnosis. Apart from hearing about the footballer Christian Erikson being fitted with one, I knew nothing about such a device. I did not know what it did, or the impact it would have on my body, or how it would be implanted, or just how much it would affect me psychologically. More research and understanding was needed.

Three days later, I was transferred to a normal cardiac award, with patients waiting for stents, pacemakers and ICDs to be fitted. The people on the ward were amazing; both the patients and the staff were incredible. I am a very fussy eater and the staff ensured I had something I liked, even if it wasn't on the menu. Talking to the other patients helped me, especially my chats with James, who was a lot younger than anyone else on the ward. He was also having an ICD fitted.

I was going to reccive a two-wire ICD from Boston

Dynamics, which would pace my heart and provide a shock if I ever needed it. An ICD is a device slightly larger than a Tic-Tac box, which is implanted under your left shoulder in a pocket created by the surgeon. It can be inserted above or under the muscle. Depending on your diagnosis, different lead setups are offered. In my case, I needed a two-lead device. This device acts as a pacemaker but will also administer a shock if required; it is basically a portable defibrillator in your chest. The device also comes with a base unit (like a broadband router) that communicates with the ICD via Bluetooth and sends diagnostics to the hospital. It even comes with a smartphone app that shows the battery life and the next download date. The ICD has a battery life of 13 years if it's not needed to administer a shock, and replacement is straightforward so long as the leads haven't deteriorated.

My ICD nurse, Trudie, explained the device and showed us a demonstration model and how it would work, where it was to be implanted and why I needed it. I was given an online link to a document from Boston Dynamics that was over 50 pages long, which detailed the problems that can occur with an ICD and other devices/situations. It was a long document to read, but very beneficial. So much misinformation is available online, so to read through something prepared by the company that developed my ICD was reassuring.

At this point, I did not know the impact it would have on my life. I did not understood that having this device would stop me from driving for six months and would trigger the critical illness cover on my life insurance. But it was a no-brainer: I had cheated death already and to know that this small device would save me if it happened again, I had to have it fitted. The recommendation from my consultant was enough; he was the expert. They would not implant these devices unless it was necessary – and having it could potentially save my life.

The surgery was scheduled for 12th April and I waited in hospital, under constant monitoring. Professor Yousef needed to be comfortable that I had understood the implications of the surgery, both physically and mentally, and that I was prepared.

I underwent an MRI scan before the operation to check my stents and ensure I was fit enough to receive the implant. During the scan, music is played through the speakers to relax you. The hospital had BBC Radio 2 playing and it was dedication time. The DJ started playing Queen's *Who Wants to Live Forever*, which made me laugh. The radiographer was also laughing – but told me to keep still as it was ruining the MRI scan.

Lying in a hospital bed, waiting for treatment can be boring, but the people on my ward were so nice. There was much laughter, much football watching via James' iPad (including the Champions League one evening, when we all pulled up chairs and watched) and I am extremely grateful to these people for making my stay a bearable one – especially James, who provided me with laughter and someone to talk to during some dark days.

Unfortunately, we had a COVID case on our ward, which meant the ward was locked down and we could not receive visitors. Mel dropped off clothes, toiletries and food, but she couldn't see me.

On the day of my operation, James went to have his ICD fitted first. When he returned to the ward, he was awake and told me that although it was painful, it had gone well and there was nothing to worry about. I was next.

I was prepared for surgery and taken down to the operating theatre, which was specially kitted out to fit ICDs and pacemakers. I was met by Professor Yousef, who explained the procedure again. He told me that, because of my condition and the cardiac arrest I had suffered, he wanted to test the device to ensure it would shock me back to life. I just had to sign the consent form for him to effectively kill me and then bring me back to life. He joked that I had probably signed hundreds of contracts with terms and conditions, but I had never signed away my life before. I was now, but I was in good hands, so I didn't hesitate.

I was put under anaesthetic and the operation began, but I woke up during the implant procedure. It was painful, and I was given more anaesthetic to put me back to sleep. I had inherited this 'ability' from my father, who had woken during a knee operation. I had also woken up during an operation on my teeth many years before, frightening the dentist!

I was transferred back to the ward and told to rest. It was strange to think that, only a few days before, I had no stents, no leads into my heart, and here I was having had two operations on it. My operation had been a success, the device had been tested and I was recovering well. It is hard to describe what it feels like to have an ICD fitted; it is strange. I don't know what I expected, but I wasn't expecting the impact that it would have on my life.

I stayed in hospital until 14th April 2022 and received fantastic care from everyone involved in the NHS. I was, however, extremely sore. With six broken ribs from the CPR, and the ICD implant, the bruising was starting to show.

On the day of discharge, I was given the base unit for the ICD and told to set it up at home. My device would download periodic updates via the base unit so any incident could be analysed quickly. Amazing technology. And then I was discharged, with an appointment scheduled for six weeks' time. I was given strict instructions not to raise my left arm above my head, and no heavy lifting, as the leads needed time to settle into my heart. It had been a very traumatic experience for both me and my family, but

I was thankful that I was still alive and able to go home. I am very lucky to have a support network at home: my wife and son could look after me, and my business would continue to function under the control of the managing director, Matt. Not everyone is so lucky.

Getting into the car and going home was an experience. My shoulder, which had a large dressing on it, was painful, and I did not want to put a seatbelt on. My wife, sister, and son, who had all come to take me home, were on full alert for any signs of discomfort. The drive from Cardiff to our home in Carmarthen took about an hour. It was very different for me to be sitting in the back of the car, as I usually did all the driving. This was something I was going to have to get used to. A six-month driving ban was about to be enforced by the DVLA because of the SCA and ICD.

BACK HOME: A TIME OF REFLECTION

On arrival home, we started to digest what had happened. Because of the COVID case on our ward, my family had not visited me, so this was the first opportunity we'd had to talk.

My diagnosis of hypertrophic cardiomyopathy (HCM) was a shock to the family. My father and brother had died of ischaemic heart disease, but we had never had a diagnosis of HCM in the family. The diagnosis meant I would need to take medication for the rest of my life and to be monitored to see if my condition changed.

Although HCM is thought to affect 1 in 500 people in the UK, I had never heard of cardiomyopathy before and was unaware of the support networks available through Cardiomyopathy UK. Of course, the first place I looked was Google. This was a mistake. There are so many sites with lots of information, much of which is not relevant to your actual condition. There are different forms of cardiomyopathy, and different stages, and each case is different. Whilst you share a common bond with other patients, you need to ensure you have the full facts from your medical practitioner.

The internet can fill your mind with all sorts of thoughts, especially when you are diagnosed. Cardiomyopathy is a serious condition, and it can be life-threatening, but it can be managed and controlled with medication.

You need also to bear in mind that I have never smoked and did not drink much alcohol at all (a lager shandy every now and then), so my lifestyle was good. I am a very fussy eater, but I was exercising regularly and showed no signs of the disease. Yet I had a blockage and my heart had gone into ventricular fibrillation (VF). I was lucky that it had been shockable. It is a strange feeling knowing that your heart was fine, had gone into VF (fast rhythm) and then just stopped. Nothing. No pulse, no heartbeat.

I now know that some people who have an SCA are not so lucky; their heart is not in a shockable state, and they cannot be brought back. Many young children playing football collapse and do not survive. It really makes you think about how fragile life is and how it can change in an instant.

If I had been walking my dogs alone, I would be dead. If I had been driving my car, I dread to think what would have happened and the carnage I could have caused, albeit out of my control.

I was now facing a life of constant medical supervision and genetic testing, as well as my son and sister being tested for the condition. I had never been ill before; I'd broken bones and had football injuries (ACL), but nothing of this nature.

Lots of thoughts were running through my mind. We had a mortgage, bills to pay, I had a job to return to. How long was my life expectancy? What was my life going to be like from now on? It was a lot to take in.

HEART ATTACK VS CARDIAC ARREST

Before the SCA, I did not know that there is a difference between a heart attack and a cardiac arrest. A heart attack is when blood flow to the heart is blocked, and sudden cardiac arrest is when the heart malfunctions and suddenly stops beating.

It was described to me as a heart attack is the plumbing, whereas a cardiac arrest is the electrical system.

A cardiac arrest leads to the heart stopping the pumping of blood around the body and you stop breathing normally.

My heartbeat had stopped abruptly and unexpectedly because of an abnormal heart rate, and I had gone into ventricular fibrillation. This causes the lower heart chambers (ventricles) to twitch (quiver) uselessly.

I was looking at the British Heart Foundation's website when I saw the headline '1 in 10 survive'. The article stated that 90% of people die as a result of an out of hospital sudden cardiac arrest. I was shocked by this number. Only 10% of people survive, and many of those suffer brain injury because of lack of oxygen, or suffer psychological issues, such as depression, anxiety and PTSD.

Some people emerge from the event with a positive outcome, increased psychological resilience and see it as a positive event in their lives – but looking at the figures and realising you were extremely lucky and that many aren't brings a wave of emotion.

As I have said before, my brother and father both died of heart attacks, my father in 1994, aged 52 (his third heart attack), and my brother in 1996, aged 31 (his first). My situation was different; I did not have their condition, ischaemic heart disease.

I now know the difference between heart attacks and cardiac arrest because of what happened to me, but many people do not know how the heart works, how to perform CPR or how to use a defibrillator. This must change. I am only here today because of the skills of the people around me, instant access to a defibrillator and the highly trained Wales Air Ambulance crews and NHS doctors and nurses.

Basic first aid and CPR needs to be taught in schools and every event needs to have access to a defibrillator and know of its location. Every minute is precious, according to suddencardiacarrest.org:

"When a person goes into cardiac arrest, oxygenated blood will slow or stop being fed to the brain. It is thought that a mere 2-3 minutes in this state is enough time for a brain injury to occur. Immediate and effective CPR can help to keep some blood circulating and give the patient the best

chance of not only surviving but also surviving with as little impairment as possible.

"When the brain is fully deprived of oxygen it is called anoxia and when only partially deprived it is hypoxia. When considering an SCA, the terms are often used interchangeably. The damage done to the brain this way is categorised as an 'acquired brain injury' (ABI) – as opposed to having a brain injury from birth.

"A good percentage of sudden cardiac arrest survivors will have experienced enough downtime to have some degree of ABI but quite often they leave the hospital without any diagnosis or care plan for it."

Without the CPR and defibrillator, I know I would either be dead or have suffered significant brain damage. It is at this point in the story that I pause to think about my son and wife. My son was witnessing this event unfold: CPR, defibrillator, air ambulances, rushing to hospital. And my wife received the phone call that I had collapsed, not knowing if I was alive or dead, not knowing what state I was in or if I was going to survive.

The effect on the people around you is massive; the impact on their lives is huge. Care is concentrated on the patient, for obvious reasons, but we must never forget the trauma of the people who help at the scene and the family who work through recovery or, sadly, must deal with the sudden death of a loved one.

Make no mistake, these events are life changing. You never go back to being the same, but you can work through it, recover, live differently, and continue to enjoy life. It is hard, I am not going to lie, and there are people significantly worse off than me. I am recovering well; others are not so lucky.

LIVING WITH AN ICD

Daily life with an ICD was going to be different. I needed advice on exercise and sports, driving (see separate chapter on driving), sexual activity, using household appliances, travelling, and medical and dental procedures to ensure they did not interfere with the device. Initially, the list was overwhelming, but it is mostly common sense.

After reading through the list and the advice, I soon realised that some occupations are almost impossible to return to; for example, car mechanics, as the alternator in a motor vehicle creates a large magnetic field and if you lean over a running car, this field can set off the alarm in the ICD and cause the ICD to report errors, which will be reported back to the hospital.

We drive an electric car and I discovered that being in the car while it was moving was OK, but not sitting in it as it charges, especially while using a fast, high-powered charger.

So far, I have not encountered any issues, although we have been careful to ensure I do not put myself in a position that might cause problems. Even after six months, I am not lifting heavy objects or typing a lot, as it causes pain in my left shoulder.

One aspect of having an ICD fitted is passing through security at certain locations. Electronic security devices can cause the ICD alarm to go off or for it to report disturbances in the electrical impulses. In severe cases, they can cause the ICD to fire inappropriately, resulting in a shock. Even the security barriers in shops can cause issues, and I had been told not to stand near them for too long. I was issued with an ICD paper that folds up into a card; I always carry it with me, as it explains that I have an ICD fitted and I give it to any security personnel when there's a need to pass through security gates. I went online and transferred this information onto a plastic card, as it was easier to fit into my wallet and was more durable than the paper version. In the USA, Boston Dynamics provides the plastic cards for free, but in the UK they don't; you have to pay for them to be made.

My first experience of using the ICD card was on a visit to the UK Prime Minister in the Houses of Parliament in London, through my work as co-founder of LABRATS International, an organisation fighting for recognition for the British nuclear veterans. I approached the security gate, took off my belt and put my belongings in the plastic container and it went through the scanner. I had my card at the ready and told the security guard that I had an ICD fitted. "No problem," he said. I went to the left of the gate, they patted me down instead, and I passed through security. I did not even show my card; they had been fully trained on security and ICDs.

I had to pass through another security checkpoint and when I told the security guard there that I had an ICD, he joked that I did not look old enough. This is now a common issue that a lot of people face: their disability is not visible; it is on the inside. People say, "You look well," which I do – I look as I always did – but I definitely do not feel the same.

I wanted to return to watching and playing football, but I was not ready to play and watching on the side-lines has the risk of being hit by a ball. Initially, my wife and I were concerned that if I was in close contact with other people (such as on the tube or in large crowds), my ICD could potentially get knocked, especially in the early months of the implant. This could dislodge the leads or cause the ICD to malfunction, shut down or deliver an inappropriate shock.

We found a fantastic protector called Vital Beat. This device sits in a pocket in an undershirt and has either one or two shields, including a sport shield. The protectors are not cheap, but they provide great protection and are supplied with a template that allows you to create your own pocket if you have some sewing skills. I asked a very good friend (Janet Barton) to add pockets to some existing T-shirts using the template; she adapted three T-shirts and I have used them to great effect.

I am yet to return to football, but I used the protector during my London trip and whilst standing on the side-lines watching football. You can visit the website (https://www.vitalbeat.com/) for more information and the products they offer for pacemakers, ICDs, S-ICDs and for children.

I was given great advice on an online support group to name my ICD, and embrace what it does and that it can save my life. So, as a family, we decided to give it a name. My wife chose 'Arnie' – as in *The Terminator* – as it brought me back. Arnie is now part of the family and will be part of me for the rest of my life.

MEDICATION

When I left hospital, I was given a cocktail of medication to take. Everyone's medication is different, but I was sent home with:

- Ramipril 1.25mg twice a day
- Prasugrel 10mg once a day
- Bisoprolol 2.5mg once a day
- Atorvastatin 80mg once a day
- Dispersible aspirin 75mg once a day

I was told that due to the medication, I may feel tired and get a dry, tickly cough, which is a side effect of Ramipril. The Prasugrel was because of having two stents fitted and would be reviewed after twelve months. Bisoprolol is a beta-blocker, which slows the heartbeat and decreases blood pressure. Atorvastatin is part of a group of drugs called statins, which work by reducing the amount of cholesterol made by the liver. The aspirin was given to help thin my blood.

Taking medication on a regular basis was totally new to me. Before my SCA, I had taken medicine periodically throughout my life for different conditions, but this medication was with me for life. Ensuring I had enough medication, ordering repeat prescriptions and remembering to take the pills in the morning and at the end of each day would become part of my daily routine.

It is at this point that I must explain that in Wales, where I live, medication administered via a prescription is provided free of charge by the NHS. In England, this is not the case, and I am aware that other countries have different medical fees, especially the USA.

It is essential that I keep my medication topped up and take it at regular intervals. Our local doctor's surgery (Meddygfa Tywi in Nantgaredig) is fantastic: repeat prescriptions are administered within 48 hours and they have been very supportive. Doctor Hern called me one evening after receiving my notes from the hospital to ask how I was, ensure I was OK and reassure me that if I needed anything I could reach out to him. He also put me on the risk register, so I am now invited to receive regular inoculations, such as the pneumonia jab, which I chose to take in July.

All drugs have side effects and can affect people differently. What works for one patient may not work for another, so if you are feeling unwell after taking medication, see your doctor. It took me a while to get used to my medication, but with perseverance, your body gets used to it.

I will now be on regular doses of medication for the rest of my life and I'll receive regular check-ups from both the doctor and the hospital. My medication may change over time – one tablet I am taking is scheduled for a review in 12 months so they may reduce it, but it depends on my condition and how I am reacting to the tablets.

I purchased a weekly planner for the pills and ensure it is topped up, with the medication sorted into mornings and evenings. I would encourage anyone who must take medication to get one. My memory is not as good as it was before my SCA and the planner allows me to see instantly if I have taken my tablets, as sometimes I cannot remember. This is especially useful when I am not at home, such as when travelling.

If you have a carer, these medication planners are great for planning a week or month's medication, especially when there are different dosages and different tablets at different times.

DRIVING & DVLA

I passed my driving test in September 1988. I was 17 years old. Since then, I have always held a driving licence and had access to a car. UK law states that as I'd had an out of hospital sudden cardiac arrest and an ICD that was not implanted as a precautionary measure, I would lose my driving licence for six months. If the ICD is fitted as a precautionary measure, the driving ban is only one month. Not all countries have the same laws; it is different for each country and done on a case-by-case basis.

I was not aware of this when I chose to have the ICD fitted, but even if I had known, it would not have made a difference to my choice. The consultant recommended an ICD, and I took his advice.

For anyone who drives, the freedom that a driving licence brings cannot be described until it is taken away. Thirty-four years of driving and now I was banned.

I was told to surrender my licence to DVLA (Drivers Vehicle Licencing Authority, the government department in the UK that governs driving), and I sent my licence off in the post. When the six months is up, I would be able to drive under Section 88, which meant I would not have to wait for my licence to be reissued and I could drive whilst the application was being processed.

After surrendering my licence, I received a letter from DVLA telling me they had revoked it due to dizziness or fainting! I wrote back explaining the situation, and received a very quick reply that included the details of my ICD. However, it also said that if my ICD fired and I received a shock within the first six months of the implant, the ban would be for two years from the date of the shock.

So, the family and I are hoping that I do not receive a shock so I can return to driving. If I receive a shock after the initial six months, I will be banned again for a further six months. I hope I will never need the ICD to shock me, but I am reassured that if I did need it, the device will save me.

I am now completely reliant on my wife Mel to drive me and Joseph everywhere. It is not something that I thought would happen to me at the age of 51! This is where I am extremely lucky. My wife has taken Joseph and me to football matches, doctors' appointments, haircuts, school, and many other appointments. Only once have we needed to rely on public transport; it was very frustrating waiting around to be picked up, especially as I live in a remote area where I cannot catch a bus or walk into town without crossing a dual carriageway, which is impossible.

Other friends have also picked up Joseph and me for football events and we are extremely grateful to Martin, who has ensured I have not missed watching the football team train and play.

Without my driver's licence, I am also unable to work. I need to travel for my work to respond to emergency situations. So, I must decide if I am to return to work after my initial six months recovery or if I am to take a different path and retrain, or retire and continue my voluntary work. It comes down to money: can I afford not to work, and will my condition allow me to work?

If I am honest, I was not fit to drive during the first three months of my recovery. I was falling asleep a lot and I had some bad days when I was in bed for most of the day. I have come to terms with my six-month ban; it is a consequence of my SCA and ICD implant and it is very inconvenient, but it is a very small price to pay to be alive. It is frustrating not being able to drive, though. Being independent for 34 years and now reliant on my wife and other people is difficult.

I cannot imagine the impact that the loss of driving entitlement would have on someone who relies on driving for a career, such as an HGV driver. Their career would be over, and their income would be reduced to zero. It makes you realise how your life can change in an instant.

I will need to re-apply for my licence using a D1 form and it will be my cardiologist who signs to state that I am fit to drive. I have been told to apply at least six weeks before the due date, so the application can be processed by DVLA to avoid any delays as they are working through a backlog of cases.

The day that I can drive again will be great. It will be another step on my road to recovery. My entitlement to drive larger vehicles will be reduced, but it will be a relief if the first six months passes without my ICD firing.

~

UPDATE: I have now received confirmation that rather than being suspended, my licence was revoked. This means I cannot drive until I have a letter from the DVLA and my physical licence. The D1 form and the DEFIB form have been completed early (apparently you can apply up to eight weeks in advance of the six-month anniversary of the date of your ICD fitment) and my cardiologist has signed me off as fit to drive. I just hope DVLA are quick to process my application.

REACHING OUT

Included in my leaving pack from the hospital was a leaflet for Cardiomyopathy UK, a charity that provides support for people suffering from all types of cardiomyopathy. I was very keen to research my condition and ensure I was fully aware of how it would affect me and my family going forward.

Online, we found support groups, many of which offer online sessions. I understand that reaching out is not for everyone, but I found that it helped a great deal. Google can be full of information that is incorrect; these groups include experts in their fields and can provide great support.

I was not a person who sought help, generally; I had never needed help from health professionals or insurance companies. I had worked all my life, I owned my own business and I had been self-sufficient.

We men do not express our feelings, we do not want to call out for help, and I was in completely new territory. Having never claimed any financial support from the UK Government in any capacity, I now needed to delve into the new world of benefits help. I talked to colleagues who had reached out for help and they advised me that the benefits scheme is difficult to navigate, and it can be a very long-winded process.

I needed help to claim benefits and life insurance critical illness cover, help to understand my condition, and help with understanding my new limitations. Fortunately, there is a lot of help available.

I was lucky to have a critical illness and income protection policy to help me with finances, but I was unprepared for the amount of paperwork and telephone calls it would take to ensure I claimed the money I was entitled to and could support my family.

Most people are not prepared for such a life-changing episode. In a way, the process would have been easier if I had not survived. You must be prepared for frustration, disappointment and stress. No one will meet your timeframes. It takes a lot longer than you expect and there is no compassion within the large companies, especially the insurance companies.

Not everyone is ready to reach out, but sometimes it is essential and necessary. Make sure you are receiving all the benefits you are entitled to. Your condition may allow you to claim certain benefits and access services that you are unaware of.

There is a whole world of support out there, with people willing to give you as much help as you need. If you are like me and do not want to reach out, please do not hesitate. Do it. There are so many great organisations with incredible volunteers who will support and guide you through the maze of information. It can be difficult but do it; you will not regret it.

I never thought I would be classed as disabled, but I have now come to terms with it. My condition limits what I can do, and I have accepted that. I have also found other people who share my condition, have been living with it longer than I have and have great knowledge about it, which can be a comfort.

FINANCES

Money rules everything we do, and every one of us has bills to pay. Mortgage, rent, cars, food, utilities… the list is endless.

When your source of income is suddenly switched off, it can have a major impact on your life. Losing a source of income can be extremely difficult. It can create a very stressful situation and have an effect on the whole family.

In the UK, for absence longer than four days from work, you need a sick note. This allows your employer to claim Statutory Sick Pay from the government and pay you the current rate, which is, at the time of writing (August 2022), £99.35 per week. An employer can pay this for up to 28 weeks.

However, I was not employed; I run my own business. I had a contract with a client that I was expected to fulfil. Unfortunately, no one else within the business was qualified to continue the contract, so it had to end. This was a large sum of money and losing it was a big loss to the business. For many people who have had similar health problems, the impact of losing the main source of household income can cause major stress and worry – which my consultant had told me to avoid.

When I purchased my house, my mortgage advisor recommended I take out critical illness cover and income protection as I was effectively self-employed. This advice has ensured that I can keep my house and my family can stay in the property.

I was also lucky to have savings to fall back on and, with the life assurance cover, I was reassured that I would be financially stable in the short to medium term, even though life would not be the same. But it is hard – it can be a real struggle and when you need immediate help, it can be difficult to find. The process of applying for benefits and life insurance pay-outs takes time.

Not everyone has savings. Many people live month to month on their salaries and they have children to consider, loans and other financial commitments. Without support, it can be easy to spiral into debt and the stress this causes can affect your condition.

As I said in the previous chapter, reaching out and asking for help is not a weakness. In the UK, the benefit system is there to help you and there are organisations, including many charities, that can help you too, depending on your circumstances.

Everyone's financial situation is different. You may not need to ask for help, you may have enough money to see you through this difficult time, but there are still things you can claim, such as a disabled railcard or a blue badge for parking. These two items alone will save you time and money.

Financial strain can cause many issues, especially stress, which should be avoided at all costs. My advice is to not bury your head in the sand. Reach out to organisations and ensure you are claiming any benefits you are entitled to.

Financial security cannot be taken for granted and an incident such as an SCA will impact the whole family, especially if it happens to the main breadwinner. Check your insurance policies and see if they will cover you in the event of illness.

LIFE INSURANCE

As I mentioned, when I bought my current house in 2017, I had great financial advice from Bradley, a mortgage advisor from a company called CMME. They specialise in arranging mortgages for self-employed people and business owners whose income is not straightforward. Bradley recommended we take out life insurance with critical illness cover as well as income protection, which would cover the mortgage payments if I was unable to work at any point.

At the time, I had no health issues, but both my family medical history and that of my wife's family was not good. Bradley informed us that the insurance would cost more each month because of this, but it would be very beneficial to take it out.

We applied and one insurance company covered me, and another covered my wife. The premiums were high but affordable – and, as it turned out, well worth it.

While I was in hospital, Mel spoke to Bradley, who sent over the details of the policies and how to claim. Mel called them and told them about my condition and the ICD and we were sent the claim forms.

I own a business and I am effectively self-employed, with a salary and dividends paid through the business, so my case was more complex than most people employed by a business. However, I was not prepared for the length of time the insurance company took to pay out my claim.

Two policies, both with the same company but dealt with by different departments. Mel and I filled out the claim forms and sent all the information to the insurance company via email.

The insurer then informed us that they needed to speak to my doctor, and they sent out further forms for the critical illness cover, which the doctor filled in and sent back within a few days. However, the income protection forms, which needed to be returned within a month, took a few weeks. We called the doctor's surgery, only to be told that the person dealing with them was away on holiday. They were eventually completed, after we visited the surgery to ensure they had been filled in, but unfortunately, my doctor sent everything in the post, rather than via email.

After hearing nothing from the insurance company, I telephoned the critical illness team to be told that they had a backlog of four weeks before they would even look at the forms; this was because of COVID and a lack of staff to process claims. I was shocked that a company would be this far behind on their claims and that they would not even be looking at the forms to see if they required any further information, but there was nothing I could do.

It was during one phone call that the representative told me I could request a call back from my caseworker. Under their current standards, the caseworker would have to call me back within five days, which would circumvent the four-week wait. Of course, I took up this offer. After speaking to the caseworker, the claim was looked at much sooner than if I had waited the four weeks. I don't think that representative was meant to tell me this shortcut; they probably felt sorry for me or wanted to get my case closed, as I called them regularly.

A few weeks after the call with my caseworker, my claim was approved. Because of the amount of money they were paying me (which was to clear my mortgage), it had to be signed off by a senior employee. I had also lodged a complaint regarding the length of time and the backlog of cases, which was accepted, and further compensation was paid. The staff at the insurance company were excellent; they were just overloaded with cases and were themselves under pressure.

We paid off the mortgage and now had to concentrate on the income protection claim, which is designed to pay out a regular income if you are incapacitated from work after a fixed period, which in my case was three months.

Each Monday, I would call the income protection team to progress my case. They must have been extremely fed up with me. Then I received a message stating that they wanted further information relating to my tax returns; this was after waiting over 14 weeks. I sent it immediately.

Again, I waited and then called them to speak to a representative who told me he would take personal charge and call back within three days. On the third day, I called them and spoke to a manager who told me that my claim had been approved and payments would now commence monthly, with any arrears being paid within three days. He told me to wait for the paperwork.

Four days passed and I telephoned to ask about the paperwork as I had not received any notification. After complaining, the notification was received a few minutes later via email. Payment was also received direct to my bank account. The process had taken four months to complete.

For anyone who has lost their income and their livelihood, the stress of paying bills is incredible. We had some income and savings, but for many, this is not the case. To be told that you have a claim and it is valid, but it will not be looked at for four weeks and then it may not be fully approved if further information is required, is extremely stressful. For most people, paying a mortgage is their highest expense each month and you need to ensure you have enough funds to cover the payment.

I cannot emphasise how stressful this situation was for me, especially as my cardiologist had told me to avoid stress! I understand the process the companies must go through, checking paperwork and ensuring the claim is genuine, and I might just have been unlucky, but the time taken to process my claim was ridiculous.

If you are reading this and have no insurance at all, get some: whatever you can afford. It is critical, especially for the self-employed or people on zero-hour contracts. My condition has meant that I have had to give up a contract that paid well and covered my bills. I am now mortgage free, which has helped us, and the income protection is providing support until I return to work, whenever that might be. I would have had to return to work too soon or sell my house if I had not had the insurance cover.

At the time of writing, we are in a cost-of-living crisis here in the UK, with fuel and groceries increasing in price. The advice I received from Bradley has saved us. It was stressful getting the claims approved, but we would have had to change our lives completely without the insurance.

I understand that if you are reading this book an SCA or heart problem may already have occurred, but it is still not too late to act. Check policies and take out new ones to ensure you can live without financial stress if anything else is to happen. We do not like to think of our own mortality, but we must ensure that our loved ones are cared for, we have provision for funeral plans and we are financially secure when something happens that affects our income and capacity to work.

UK BENEFITS

Until now, I had never claimed UK benefits in my lifetime. I have worked since I was 15 years old, and I've run a business since 1996, when I was 25. Friends who have claimed benefits told me that claiming was a nightmare, a minefield of forms and misinformation. They were right!

Each country is different when it comes to claiming benefits and I can only comment on my own experience in the UK, but I am assuming the process is similar in every country and application forms must be completed.

After my SCA, I was immediately put on sick leave by my doctor, initially for three months and then for six months. So, the business paid me Statutory Sick Pay, which is a flat fee of £99.35 per week for up to 28 weeks. This figure was not enough to cover food for the family for a week, never mind any household bills. It was a real shock to lose a good income and replace it with this low amount.

I was advised by my nurse to claim Personal Independence Payment (PIP) and apply for a disabled blue badge for the car and, if my PIP claim was successful, a disabled railcard. A lot to take in. If I did not return to work after six months and the SSP stops and I was unemployed, I was told to claim Employment Support Allowance (ESA). There are also other top-up benefits that can be applied in certain cases and each one has its own application process. My friend was right: it was a minefield!

So, on the advice of my nurse, we started with PIP and applied online to see if I was eligible. They reviewed my application and I received a letter in the post requesting a telephone assessment of my condition to accompany the information from my medical file. I had been told to wait six weeks for this appointment, but it was scheduled within four.

I spoke to a very nice lady on the telephone, explained my situation and answered her questions about my mobility and medication. Please bear in mind that I had been diagnosed with cardiomyopathy after my SCA, so I had an underlying incurable condition, which obviously enhanced my claim. As I have stated before, everyone is different, so PIP might not be awarded to everyone.

After the call, I was informed that it could take up to six weeks to assess my claim and decide on a payment if I was eligible. However, it was only two weeks later that I received the assessment letter, and I was awarded PIP – not at the highest level, but it was still an award. It had not been a nightmare and the process was relatively simple and a lot faster than I expected; a completely different experience to the insurance claim.

I also applied for a disabled blue badge – for anyone not in the UK, this is a parking permit that enables you to park in disabled spaces. Again, the application process was online. My doctor phoned a few days later to speak to me about my condition and how it was affecting me as he had seen the notes from the hospital and Carmarthen Council had asked him to sign off my blue badge application, which he was happy to do. I waited for a response from Carmarthen Council, which I assumed would be positive as my doctor had approved it. Unfortunately, the council declined my application.

The letter informed me that I could appeal, so I did so in writing and spoke to a member of the team, who then told me that my appeal had been successful, and my blue badge would be approved for a year and then reviewed. This badge has enabled us to park closer to shopping centres, train stations and other areas and has been incredibly helpful, as initially walking long distances was difficult. It is now easing, and I do not anticipate renewing the badge in a year's time, but we will have to wait and see if my condition deteriorates, in which case I will need it. It has been very useful.

As I was now receiving PIP, I was entitled to a disabled railcard, which would discount any travel by a third for myself and another adult travelling with me. This is a considerable saving as I would be using the train for some of my travels, especially during the six-month driving ban.

Again, the application was online. I applied and sent a copy of my PIP approval letter, paid my £54 for three years (you can pay £20 per year) and, two weeks later, my railcard appeared. We have already used it to book trains to Liverpool for a conference and recouped the money of the railcard in one trip!

Initially, we thought that as I had been approved for a disabled blue badge, I would automatically be entitled to a disabled railcard, but this is not the case. It was only because I receive PIP that I was able to apply.

I never saw myself being disabled. I was fit and healthy and, apart from a few football injuries (broken bones and an anterior cruciate ligament snap, which required surgery), I had not been seriously ill. Coming to terms with your limitations can take some time. Rushing back to work, thinking you can still do everything you did before, is difficult. I will get back to near my pre-SCA condition, but I must be patient and it is hard, both mentally and physically.

My six months Statutory Sick Pay runs out in October 2022 and as I am not ready to return to work, I will need to apply for ESA to add to my income, which will be up to £77 per week. Without the critical illness cover and the income protection policy, we would have needed to totally re-evaluate our income and expenditure and decide if I needed to return to work.

At present, we have turned down contracts and I have given up my role as a Data Protection Officer as I was required to respond to emergency situations within 72 hours and visit anywhere in the UK to assess and write up reports. With my fatigue and not being able to drive, this was impossible to do.

It was time to decide whether to retrain into a role that better suited my condition, or retire. I needed more information from my doctor. I am not ready to return to work; the physical and mental aspects are still too much. I am still falling asleep at different points in the day, mainly in the afternoons, and pushing through on one day really affects the next day, when I am tired. Concentrating on a serious data breach is something I can no longer manage.

That is why this book exists; I wrote it to fill a gap of doing nothing. I wanted to be proactive within the new community I find myself in; I wanted to help other people and raise awareness as much as possible. Not for me, but for the 90% who don't make it. Perhaps my experience could help someone who has just experienced their SCA or been diagnosed with a heart condition that will affect them forever.

So, my advice is to apply for the benefits. Do not be too proud. If you are entitled, they will be paid to you. It can be a minefield, but there are lots of people who can help you, people who have been through what you are experiencing. Just ask for help.

VISITING THE TEAM

My wife had already been to visit the football team and had thanked them for saving me, but I wanted to go and visit them during a training session to show my gratitude for saving my life and ensuring that I had a future with my family.

I felt OK in the first few days after returning from hospital. The bruising on my arm and chest was severe and it was difficult to move around and especially to cough or sneeze, but I was determined to show them that I was recovering and that I would return to play again one day.

Travelling in the car was difficult. The seat belt on the passenger side of the car came across my left shoulder (our steering wheel is on the right in the UK) and it rested directly on the ICD and the scar, so I sat in the back of the car on the opposite side until I felt comfortable with the seat belt.

I had not travelled anywhere since my journey home from hospital, and it was good to get out and get some fresh air. The trip was a short 10-minute car ride to the training ground. It felt strange not being able to drive and to be sitting in the back of a car, so this was a new experience, one I knew I would have to endure for six months.

When we arrived at the ground, we met everyone and thanked them for their support and for returning my car back home from Caldicot Leisure Centre, where it had been left. Everyone was glad to see me, and I spoke to Sean, shook his hand and told him I could never do enough to thank him for what he did for me and my family. Not everyone can administer CPR; not everyone is brave enough to take charge and do it. Along with Martin, Sean's quick actions had kept the blood flowing around my body and saved me from brain damage through lack of oxygen. He was very humble, said it was no problem and that he was just glad I was OK, recovering well and out of hospital.

It was a good feeling to sit and watch the team train and to feel somewhat back to normal, albeit not playing. To be involved in a team with great colleagues who had gone above and beyond was extremely uplifting.

For anyone who has played a team sport, humour plays a large part in the team spirit. I was asked by one player if I remembered the incident. I told them that I remembered travelling to the tournament, getting changed into the team kit and nothing else. He remarked, "That's good, because you played rubbish in the first game." Then he laughed and said, "Only joking!"

To have a team of people who helped the family,

who made sure my son and wife were looked after, is something I shall always be grateful for. Not only the football team that I played for, but neighbours, friends, and the parents of Joseph's football team, who were all very supportive.

It is during emergencies like these that you realise your circle of friends and family is an incredible support. People really do step up and help you. There is great compassion within this world, and it is invaluable in situations where emotions are running high.

I am so glad I visited the team early; it was good for me, and for the rest of the team to see me. I have since watched many training sessions and a tournament and I do hope to play again once the doctors give me the OK to return to training. I feel it is important for me. My wife is not so keen on me returning to physical activity yet, but she understands the importance of it, not only for good cardio rehab, but for me mentally.

RETURNING TO THE FOOTBALL TOURNAMENT

The football tournament that I had my SCA at was cancelled following the incident and a new date had been arranged six weeks later. I wanted to watch the team play in a competitive match, so Martin arranged to pick me up for the trip to Neath.

The tournament started and a member of another team came over to our manager, Josh, and asked him: "How is your player that collapsed?"

Josh replied, "You can ask him yourself. He is here!" The player was so surprised to see me and was overjoyed that I was OK.

It had not entered my mind that the players at this tournament would be the same players who were at the tournament where I had my SCA. Word quickly spread, and I was soon shaking hands with hundreds of players, many who could not believe that I was there, only six weeks after my SCA. It was very humbling to have players I had not met wishing me well and saying they were very happy I had survived.

This experience made me realise the impact my SCA had, not only on my family, but also on complete strangers who witnessed the event. I had not realised how much my SCA had impacted a whole community. Some players told me had been wondering for weeks if I had survived and it was the first thing on their mind when they came to play in the tournament.

One player told me he had written to the organisers of the tournament, expressing his concern that they had been lucky that a defibrillator was present at the leisure centre hosting the event and that they needed to ensure one was available at every tournament, ready to be used if necessary. He was an ex-paramedic and understood the importance of a defibrillator being available as they save lives.

On returning from the tournament, I reflected on the day. I never imagined my SCA had made such an impact on so many people. I knew I needed to research my condition further in order to help as much as possible.

I know not everyone would want to go back to the scene of their SCA, but it was extremely beneficial for me to return to the tournament. I am still involved with the football community, and I am now helping with coaching Joseph's team. It's low impact activity, but it enables me to keep in contact with the game, which is invaluable to me; it also allows me to spend more time with my son.

DEFIBRILLATOR AND CPR

After returning home and the conversation with the ex-paramedic at the Neath walking football tournament, we realised that if anything was to happen to another member of the team, we may not have access to a defibrillator and many of us had not been trained in CPR.

Martin was very keen to ensure that all the members of the team that required it were trained in CPR and he knew a retired nurse who could give us the training.

Mel and I discussed the possibility of funding a portable defibrillator for the team that could be taken to training and matches, ensuring it was available not just to our team members, but to anyone who needed it. As directors of ICARIS Ltd, we decided sponsorship of the defibrillator was possible and would be paid for by the company.

We informed Josh, the coach, what we wanted to do and researched the best portable defibrillators. Then we transferred the funds to the team to purchase one. These defibrillators are not cheap – in the UK they cost around £1200 – but you cannot put a price on saving someone's life.

Martin arranged for the retired nurse to perform CPR training and members of the team attended a session instead of football training.

For anyone who has completed CPR training, you will appreciate that giving CPR is a hard task. It can be tiring providing it for a long period of time and you must be able to take charge of the situation and ensure that, if needed, you can hand over to another person.

Before the session started, the nurse took me to one side and asked if I was OK with the training and if she could mention my case. She said that if it got too much for me, Mel or Joseph were to tell her and she would stop the course.

She provided excellent training on CPR, using the dummy. You do not realise how hard you must press on a person's chest to get through to the heart; it is physically draining. Our instructor was very knowledgeable. She explained different scenarios and answered questions from the team.

We then were instructed on how to use the defibrillator, something that many of us had not thought about. The defibrillator we had purchased was a smart unit, which meant that after setting it up and connecting the pads, it would check the heart to see if a shock was possible and would not administer one if it was not necessary. The unit talks you through every step to ensure you can administer a shock, even if you haven't been trained.

We were instructed on what not to do when

attaching a defibrillator, especially making sure that no one is touching the patient whilst the unit is analysing the heart, as it can pick up rhythms from the person holding the patient. This information was invaluable to us.

By the end of the session, everyone understood how to administer CPR and how to work the defibrillator. It was emotional for me, Mel and Joseph at times, but I felt it was essential that, as a team, we knew the correct procedure, just in case it was ever to happen again.

I would recommend everyone undergoes this training. Both CPR and defibrillator training should be taught in schools and to everyone as basic first aid. Without there being someone trained in CPR, I would either be dead or severely brain damaged now. Without the defibrillator to get my heart going again, the CPR would have needed to be completed for 20 minutes, which is extremely difficult for anyone to do.

After reading this book, if you can do one thing, undergo the training. If you are involved in a community activity, get people trained and ensure you know where the nearest defibrillator is, no matter where you are. It certainly saves lives; it saved mine.

It is a sobering thought when you consider that when cardiac arrest occurs, cardiopulmonary resuscitation (CPR) must be started within two minutes. After three minutes, global cerebral ischemia – the lack of blood flow to the entire brain – can lead to brain injury that gets progressively worse. By nine minutes, severe and permanent brain damage is likely. After 10 minutes, the chances of survival are low.

Even if a person is resuscitated, eight out of every ten will be in a coma and sustain some level of brain damage. Simply put, the longer the brain is deprived of oxygen, the worse the damage will be.

Some 90% of people who go into cardiac arrest outside of a hospital – meaning at home, work, or wherever it occurs – will die. Even when the heart is restarted and blood flow begins delivering oxygen to the cells again, most people will be seriously impacted. These impacts, like memory loss or mobility issues, are worse the longer the brain is deprived of oxygen.

VISITING THE AIR AMBULANCE

As I mentioned earlier, I received care from the team at Wales Air Ambulance, who sent two helicopters to help me. As part of their support package, I was contacted by Julie, the patient liaison officer for the charity. We had an initial meeting in which we discussed the incident, how I was progressing and the support they offered.

Part of this process was a timeline of events, which was available if I wanted to see what had happened to me, as I had no memory of the incident. This is optional – you don't have to know – but after talking it through with Mel, we decided it would be good for both of us to fill in the blanks. Whilst we as a family found this beneficial, I completely understand that it is not for everyone. Some people would rather not know what happened; for others who have lost a loved one, it may be too much to relive the event.

The timeline was as follows.

A 999 call was made at 10:52 after I became pale and then collapsed whilst talking to my friend at the side of the football pitch. Initially, I was breathing, and

I was put into the recovery position.

I then went into cardiac arrest and CPR was commenced immediately, while a defibrillator was being obtained and the air ambulance critical care team was dispatched from Cardiff.

After three rounds of CPR, the defibrillator was applied and three shocks were delivered. My heart began beating again and I was put into the recovery position just as the air ambulance team arrived at the football pitch at 11:12.

Twenty minutes after the 999 call, the ambulance team were at my side, having flown from Cardiff to Caldicot. This is an incredible service showing incredible dedication from an incredible team of professionals.

Two critical care practitioners carried out a rapid assessment and found that I needed help with my breathing. I was not regaining consciousness, and I was becoming agitated and clenching my jaw tightly. The team called for a second air ambulance team, to include a critical care doctor as they needed to give me a general anaesthetic and put me on a ventilator.

While waiting for the second team to arrive, they began to stabilise me. They gave me some strong sedatives to relax me so they could help me breathe more easily. They carried out a blood test and prepared all the equipment for the next stage.

At 11:55, the second helicopter arrived from Llanelli and they immediately gave me a general anaesthetic. I was then placed on a breathing machine. They carried out a tracing of my heart, which showed that the electrical signals were abnormal and I needed urgent treatment from a specialist cardiology centre.

I was transferred by road ambulance, which was mobile at 12:08, and taken to the University Hospital of Wales, arriving at 12:45.

In just under two hours, I had gone into cardiac arrest, received a shock from a defibrillator, had two air ambulances and a road ambulance attend, been sedated, given a general anaesthetic and put on a ventilator. Everyone involved is a life saver.

It was a shock to hear just how poorly I had been. I knew it was bad, but as I did not remember anything until I woke up in hospital, I hadn't understood the seriousness of my situation. My heart had stopped, I had effectively died – I was flat-lining – and it was only because of my teammates, the accessibility of a defibrillator, and the skills of the Wales Air Ambulance crew and the doctors and nurses at the hospital that I survived.

As part of the follow-up, we were invited to visit the air ambulance crew at the charity's headquarters, where we could see a helicopter up close and discuss any problems we were facing. Mel had already spoken to one member of the team, Ruby, at the hospital but I was very keen to meet the team that had saved me. We agreed as a family that we just wanted to say thank you.

I understand that this might not be for everyone and not all organisations offer this level of personal service. Unfortunately, not everyone makes it, and the grieving process is different for us all.

Julie arranged a visit to the Llanelli base and organised it to be when Ruby was on shift. Obviously, there was no guarantee the team would be there as they were on call and may get called to an incident at any time.

We travelled the 20 minutes from our home. Joseph also came as he wanted to understand more about what had happened. We were met by Julie, who gave us a copy of our timeline, explained the procedures and answered all our questions, of which there were many.

We then went to see the helicopter and were met by Ruby and another paramedic. We were given a tour of the helicopter and we were amazed by how little room they have within the helicopter and how much equipment and medicine they can carry.

Meeting Ruby and thanking her for saving my life was a wonderful experience. She commented that it was great to meet me as they often do not get to see the person afterwards; they find out what has happened, but often the patient does not return.

Even though they had saved me (and many others), they were extremely humble. "Just another day at work," Ruby said. "It is what we do."

These people are inspirational, and their dedication to saving lives should be rewarded and recognised. For me, saying thank you was not enough. These people save lives every day; they are the real heroes in the world and their skills and expertise make a massive difference.

So, after meeting the crew, I asked if there was anything I could help the charity with, such as fundraising or telling my story. I wanted to help as much as possible. Nothing I could do would be enough, but I wanted to try.

Julie informed me that she was holding a fundraising event at Cardiff Castle to generate interest in legacies and asked if I would come along and share my story. I was delighted to be able to give something back to help the charity.

The event was scheduled for a few weeks after our visit. The date coincided with Mel and a friend of ours (Susan) attending a concert in Cardiff, so it was perfect. Mel could drive us there and Joseph and I would return on the train.

We all attended the event at Cardiff Castle. First, we listened to Sabrina from Loosemores Solicitors, who gave advice on making a will. Then there was a demonstration from the ambulance crew on how they attend an incident and the work they undertake. This was extremely interesting as, only three months before, I had been the patient. Mel and Joseph did not watch as they found it too upsetting.

My participation was as part of a question-and-answer session, with Julie asking questions. Our session was well received by the audience, especially when they found out that only three months had passed since my SCA.

It was emotional. My voice cracked up many times, but I wanted to get through it and tell my story, to explain just how much it meant to my family that, through the professionalism and dedication of this team, I was here today.

I hope I can do much more for the charity in future. One of my teammates, Mike, has already run 100km to raise money for them, and Mel has undertaken a 10K run. Once I can drive, I hope to volunteer for them and ensure they continue to receive funding for this essential, life-saving service. They need £6 million a year to run, which is a monumental amount of money.

It is very reassuring to know that this service is available in Wales and is ensuring that lives are saved following accidents and incidents such as mine. It is an essential service, and we should all help as much as we possibly can.

VISITING CALDICOT LEISURE CENTRE

I called the leisure centre a few months after my SCA to arrange an appointment with the team who were first on the scene. Unfortunately, the message never got through and it took another few months to finally meet up with the staff who were present on the day.

My wife and I went to the centre, Mel for the first time ever and me for the first time since my cardiac arrest. I had been in contact with Justin Aylett, the duty officer, via email. The two other staff members who saved me on the day, Kirsty Burnett and Briden Whitbread, were no longer working at the centre but they made a special trip to meet us.

We stood on the field where my SCA occurred, and the staff members explained what had happened on that fateful day. It was a surreal experience, as I have no recollection of the incident.

They were in reception when one of my team mates ran in to tell them I had collapsed. Justin grabbed the bag they have ready for emergencies, which contains a HeartStart defibrillator.

Justin took over CPR from Sean and gave me

mouth to mouth, and then Briden took over. Kirsty tried to cut off my shirt, but the scissors in the pack would not cut the fabric, so she ripped it off. The defibrillator was applied and Kirsty told us that all she could think was "Please let it say yes to administering a shock," which, luckily for me, it did. At first, I thought I had only received one shock from the defibrillator but Kirsty told us I needed three to get my heart started.

As the air ambulance was landing, Justin and Briden lay over me to protect me from the downdraft of the rotor blades.

These three strangers ensured I was in a position to receive medical help and that I did not suffer any major brain damage. Early intervention is key to survival and they were shocking me within minutes of my collapse.

Kirsty showed me a photo of the two air ambulances on the field, and I was amazed to see that they had landed in a very small space. Testament to the skill of the pilots.

We presented the team with a certificate from Sudden Cardiac Arrest UK, thanking them for their efforts. Justin joked that he would never forget the face of the man he had kissed!

It is essential that leisure centres across the country have defibrillators and an emergency medical bag. It is also essential that staff are trained to use them. I was lucky that day that the three team members had been trained. Without this training, I do not think I would be alive today – or if I was, I would have severe brain damage.

The medical professionals state that a 'chain of survival' is essential if a life is to be saved. These three staff members were near the start of the chain and their early actions ensured the chain was never broken.

I will now be attending the leisure centre staff training sessions to show that the training works, the emergency equipment works, and that it saved my life. These people are life savers and should be forever referred to as such.

MEETING THE PM

As part of my work with LABRATS, we had been running a campaign entitled #lookmeintheye where we were asking the UK Prime Minister to meet nuclear veterans and their families to discuss formal medallic recognition. It would be the first official meeting with any UK prime minister.

I had been working (with the other directors of LABRATS) with the *Daily Mirror*, Susie Boniface and a working committee including a nuclear veteran, descendants, and the Labour MP Rebecca Long-Bailey.

I was informed that the meeting had now been scheduled and was to take place on 24th May, only seven weeks after my SCA. I had been working on this for over a year and was determined to attend. However, with Mel needing to stay at home to look after Joseph and the dogs, I would either need to travel alone (which Mel didn't want me to do) or have someone attend with me. My sister volunteered and her husband gave her a lift to a motorway service station halfway between Cheltenham and Carmarthen, where we met her. She then accompanied me on the train from Swansea to

London for an overnight stay, ready for the meeting the next day.

Everything was going well until we received a message while we were at Swindon station that the meeting had been cancelled. We had another meeting arranged with the creator of *Call the Midwife*, Heidi Thomas, so we decided to continue to London anyway. Rebecca Long-Bailey also invited us on a tour of the Houses of Parliament and to discuss the campaign.

After the meetings, we went home. My sister got off at Swindon to return to Cheltenham and I remained on the train until Swansea, where I was picked up by Mel and Joseph. My sister took very good care of me but, with the drive to Swansea station, train to Paddington and taxi to our hotel in Westminster, this trip to London was extremely tiring and I was wiped out. I had completed the journey to London from both Cheltenham and Peterborough on numerous occasions, and I had worked in London – but now I was struggling to make one trip. Life had changed for me.

I had not expected the trip to make me so tired. I felt OK, but it was too soon for me, and reality was sinking in that my previous life that I had taken for granted would no longer be possible, at least in the short term.

The working group for the campaign managed to reschedule the meeting with the PM as soon as possible, which was no easy task, as the Prime Minister is a very busy person, and their diary is full. However, a new date of June 8th was agreed and I had to make the trip again.

The routine was the same. We met my sister halfway between Cheltenham and Carmarthen and she stayed with us. Then we took the train from Swansea to Paddington and travelled across London to our hotel. We decided to have a meal in the hotel restaurant as I was tired from the trip. It was here that we met two veterans, one of whom was blind. I noticed his St Dunstan's badge and we spoke to them both. He was undergoing an operation on his eyes and he had to travel across London early in the morning. Whilst we were chatting, we realised they had come to the restaurant in our hotel as it was the cheapest place to have a meal. They told us that, with the cost of travel and a taxi the next day, they had exhausted their funds.

My sister and I decided to pay for their meal. It was the least we could do for the veterans to thank them for their service many years ago. It was at this point that I realised how fragile we are as human beings. Life changes in an instant, we get older, and we all need help at some point in our lives. This small act of kindness had brought a smile to two veterans' faces.

I knew the day of the meeting would be long. It was extremely hot and I was wearing my ICD protector, just in case. It was also the first time I had experienced security since having my ICD fitted, which I talked about a few chapters ago.

After entering Parliament, we were invited to watch Prime Minister's Questions (PMQs) from the Speakers' Gallery. It was very entertaining to watch it live; the noise level was a lot higher than I expected.

After a wait, we met Prime Minister Boris Johnson in his private office in Parliament. It was an historic meeting, the first ever official meeting between nuclear veterans and a prime minister. Afterwards, we went to Westminster Square for media interviews and then back to the office of Rebecca Long-Bailey for a debrief and sandwich.

Unfortunately, we missed our train home, so we had to wait at Paddington for the next available train. My sister again left the train in Swindon for her trip to Cheltenham. My train did not get in until after midnight and Mel and Joseph picked me up and drove me the 25 minutes home.

For the next few days I was extremely tired, but we were juggling social media, newspaper articles and interviews regarding the meeting. I was falling asleep in the afternoons for a few hours, and my body was aching. It took me around three days to get over a small trip to London.

If the meeting had not been so important, I would not have travelled. I was not physically or mentally ready for the challenge. I was invited to a United

Nations meeting in Vienna as a guest speaker, with all expenses paid, on 21st June, but I had to give my apologies as I was in no fit state to travel that far yet.

I have got stronger. It has taken longer than I thought, but I have realised that I must be patient. The seriousness of my SCA, diagnosis and operations is still sinking in and I've discovered that you have good days and bad days with cardiomyopathy, especially in the heat. But, with the stents clearing my arteries, my ICD ready to shock me if needed, controlling my condition with medication and understanding the condition, I am in a much better place than I was before the SCA, when I was a 'ticking time bomb' waiting to explode.

COMING TO TERMS MENTALLY AND PHYSICALLY

When you are an active person and you've never taken regular medication or been ill other than a few football injuries, it is hard to adjust to suddenly relying on medication and medical teams. When my GP received the notes from the hospital about my SCA, he phoned me because he was shocked to hear what had happened. Apart from an ear infection, I had not been to see him in years.

Realising the seriousness of what happened to me has been a very difficult journey. At first, I did not appreciate the impact the incident had on my family and friends. It was only after talking to them that I discovered they believed I was going to die or be severely brain damaged.

As I have said, I don't remember the first day or so in hospital, or the incident itself, and I am told that this is common; your brain blacks out the memories. Mel told me that when I awoke in hospital and she was allowed to be with me, I kept asking her what happened. There was a whiteboard above my bed with the words 'Cardiac Arrest' on it and I kept referring to it. Eventually, she asked the nurses to wipe it off!

We had lost my father and brother to heart problems, but I had been tested 20-odd years earlier and had no signs. It was a complete shock to the system. I had regained consciousness very quickly after my SCA, but many people spend days or even weeks in medically induced comas, mainly because of the length of time they were receiving CPR and the delay in getting a defibrillator to them. My shocks had come within minutes because one was available, and this was key to my survival.

Whilst in hospital, I was constantly monitored, and as well as the operations I had scans, X-rays, blood tests and medication. Time went quickly, even though it was difficult not having visitors because of Covid. But even then, what had happened to me had not properly registered with me.

Initially I thought that, with a few months' rest and recuperation, I would be able to resume my current job and carry on as before. Some people can continue, but with my diagnosis of cardiomyopathy and the trauma to my body, I was in for a shock. Life would never be the same again.

After I returned home, I tried doing things like watching Joseph play football, getting out and visiting people, going to the local pub for lunch, everyone asking how I was… These simple things now became massive achievements. My outlook on life had changed and things that I had been stressing about were no longer important. Just regaining my health and ensuring I did everything my consultant asked was my main priority.

I was lucky that I had great support at home and through my business, but not everyone is so lucky, and I do not know how I would have coped without the support of my family and friends, who have been fantastic.

Taking time to reflect on the incident, meeting the Caldicot leisure centre staff, the air ambulance team, speaking to health professionals, joining online support groups and talking with other people who have experienced SCAs and cardiomyopathy have helped immensely. It's inspiring knowing that other people have been through what I have, and they are coping with it; many people have gone on to do amazing things since their SCA.

I had time to reflect whilst recovering, time to sit and relax whilst the ICD implant settled, my ribs healed and the bruising subsided. You feel the same, you look the same, yet you are not the same. In your mind, you wonder what would have happened if you hadn't survived. That was it, that was my time on earth. You look back at your achievements, the ups and downs of daily life, the highs and the lows. You then realise you have a second chance. You can embrace the time you now have, time that has been extended for you and your family. Now that I had my diagnosis, my ICD and medication, I could continue my life (albeit in a different way) but I was still here – not quite the same, but still here.

Physically, the ICD settling in, the broken ribs and getting used to the medication was exhausting. Every time I sneezed or coughed, it was painful. Initially, I was aware of the ICD a lot, but after a few months, it became part of me, part of my daily routine.

My family went through hell that day, especially Joseph, who saw me collapse, CPR being administered, the air ambulances landing, and then waited in hospital not knowing if I would make it or if I would be brain damaged. It is a lot for loved ones to endure and for those who have experienced it, it is extremely painful.

Whilst I wait for my driving licence to be returned, I must rely on others, something I hate. But I realise I am no longer what I was. I will get stronger, I will return to doing certain tasks, but others are, for the moment, out of my reach.

I was always a very driven person, always busy, building businesses, working lots of hours, but I now realise my health was always the most important thing. If I had not survived my SCA, my family would have been ripped apart and the material items we purchased would be worthless.

Being patient is difficult. I find myself getting more impatient since the SCA, especially on bad days, when the fatigue is too much. But I am not giving in. I will not be the person who sits on the couch all day. I need to remain active; my brain needs to remain active.

I had been studying an MBA at the University of Wales, Trinity St David, and had reached the dissertation stage, so, after a few months of healing, I decided I could concentrate for a few hours a day on the dissertation and get it finished. I had informed my tutor about my SCA and diagnosis, and he had told me to take as much time as I needed and not to worry about the assignment.

Returning to study gave me a reason to get on with life. I researched for the dissertation, arranged interviews, and completed it within three months, and I am awaiting my result. This was something I could achieve from home.

My short-term memory is terrible, and concentration for long periods is hard; I have to stop and take breaks a lot more than I used to. It can be extremely frustrating, forgetting the small things and struggling to remember basic facts, yet able to recall events from many years ago. The brain is a very complex organ and I am told it will find new pathways.

Physically, I can do more each month. It is taking longer than I thought and I have concluded that I will not be returning to work in my previous role. However, I am determined to return to some form of work and help as many people as possible. Knowing that my experience may help others, I am going to retrain as a counsellor, something I *can* do with my condition.

My training began in October 2022 and it will take a few years to complete. This is a new chapter in my life and a chance to try something new. Mentally, this is something I must do. It will give me a new lease of life; it will engage my brain and help my recovery.

I would encourage anyone (if you are able to) to undertake something whilst they are recovering: a course or some physical fitness or a new activity. Try something you have always wanted to do but put off because of other commitments. It has helped me immensely. You can learn from new communities, meet new people and, most of all, enjoy the extended time you have been given.

ONLINE SUPPORT

There are a number of places you can get support, initially from your medical team and then through charities and organisations, online forums and groups for people who have been through the same experience.

My initial advice to you is not to Google your symptoms. I Googled 'Sudden Cardiac Arrest' whilst in hospital (to try and find out the difference between a heart attack and a cardiac arrest) and I was presented with this (from www.heart.org):

What is cardiac arrest?

Sudden cardiac arrest occurs suddenly and often without warning. It is triggered by an electrical malfunction in the heart that causes an irregular heartbeat (arrhythmia). With its pumping action disrupted, the heart cannot pump blood to the brain, lungs and other organs. Seconds later, a person loses consciousness and has no pulse. Death occurs within minutes if the victim does not receive treatment.

Whilst completely true, reading this only days after suffering an SCA was frightening. Google is a great tool, but there are better options, especially in the early days when everything is new.

Whilst I was in hospital, my cardiology nurse gave

us a leaflet with details of a UK charity called Cardiomyopathy UK. I searched on Facebook and joined their support group. I also found other groups for Sudden Cardiac Arrest and ICD patients.

Scrolling through the groups and reading the hundreds of posts with questions and the thousands of answers and messages of support was very reassuring. I was not alone with my condition, and the SCA survivor community was extremely supportive.

It is very easy to pick up misinformation online. Within these groups I have found not only the support incredible, but the information provided extremely helpful, especially in the early months, when you are still raw from the SCA and diagnosis. Cardiomyopathy UK has a support nurse available every day who will answer any question and signpost you where possible. This professional support, along with support from other people who have been through the same things as you, is extremely uplifting. From just chatting about life to specialist information on different aspects (ICD/HCM/DCM etc.), there is so much support out there on the internet.

Obviously, not everyone can get online – not everyone has a smartphone, tablet or computer – but it is worth the investment in the technology to spend a few hours in these groups. There is no pressure to speak; you can turn off your camera if you want to, and just listen. You'll find a list of support groups in the chapter on advice at the end of this book

I wanted to get back to normal as soon as possible, but listening to the groups, I realised that it would take time and I needed to be patient. There would be good days and bad days and I needed to heal, both physically and mentally. I will never be the same. I will try and get to the level I was before my SCA and diagnosis, but I must be realistic and take it slowly and not push myself. I like to think of myself as still in the recovery phase, getting stronger every day, performing more activities, and enjoying the simple things in life. I try not to get stressed, which can be difficult, but my mind always returns to 'Be thankful, you have been granted an extension on your life. Is it worth it?'

UNDERSTANDING CARDIOMYOPATHY

As well as understanding that I had suffered an SCA and had two stents fitted, the diagnosis of cardiomyopathy came as a shock. Nobody (as far as I was aware) had been diagnosed with cardiomyopathy in my family. My father and brother had ischaemic heart disease which caused their heart attacks, but no other diagnosis.

If I am honest, I had only heard of cardiomyopathy a few months before my SCA when a close friend was diagnosed with dilated cardiomyopathy (DCM). I did not know the difference between the different types or the difference between atrial fibrillation and ventricular fibrillation. My secondary school biology gave me the basics, but beyond that, it was a mystery.

My cardiology nurse explained my condition and how it was affecting my heart. My condition was diagnosed as: *Asymmetrical thickening of the interventricular septum. LV wall thickness: apex: 7-8 mm mid LV: Free wall 7-8 mm, septum 11 mm Basal LV: Anterior/lateral 8-9 mm, inferior 11-12 mm, septum up to 17 mm.*

I was at the start of my cardiomyopathy journey and the thickness was less than others I had spoken to but, combined with blocked arteries requiring stents and an SCA, it was a little unusual. In fact, it was described as 'the perfect storm'.

Utilising the Cardiomyopathy UK website and the support groups and meetings and chatting with the nurses was a great help. Their website is full of useful information and provides practical support on topics such as benefits, driving, life insurance and returning to work.

A very good description of HCM can be found at www.heart.org:

Hypertrophic cardiomyopathy is most often caused by abnormal genes in the heart muscle. These genes cause the walls of the heart chamber (left ventricle) to become thicker than normal.

The thickened walls may become stiff, and this can reduce the amount of blood taken in and pumped out to the body with each heartbeat.

HCM is a chronic disease that can get worse over time. This can lead to poorer function and quality of life, long-term complications, and more financial and social burden.

People with HCM may need to make lifestyle changes, such as limiting their activity, to adjust for their disease.

Hypertrophic cardiomyopathy is most often inherited and is the most common form of genetic heart disease. It can happen at any age, but most receive a diagnosis in middle age.

It's estimated that 1 in every 500 people have HCM, but a large percentage of patients are undiagnosed. Of those diagnosed, two-thirds have obstructive HCM and one-third have non-obstructive HCM.

My diagnosis was given after scans and an ECG (echocardiogram). It is recommended that siblings and children are also scanned to ensure they are not suffering with the condition. Joseph was immediately booked in for an ECG, which took place a few weeks after I was released from hospital. His results were excellent and he currently shows no sign of cardiomyopathy.

My sister was also put forward for an ECG. Unfortunately, the wait time on the NHS in England is significant, over six months before a scan could be scheduled. We were fortunate enough to have funds available to pay for a private scan, which also came back clear.

I should explain that we could not wait for the NHS scan because my sister suffered a heart attack many years ago, so she was extremely anxious about the possibility of cardiomyopathy. The anxiety of waiting and not knowing is awful.

During my stay in hospital, I had 12 vials of blood taken for genetic testing. This would inform me if I had the gene that causes cardiomyopathy. I'm still awaiting the results, but if I do have the gene, there will be further testing for other members of my family.

Understanding my condition and the fact that I could have passed it on to my son was difficult to come to terms with. But knowing it was a possibility meant at least he could get tested and we could deal with any problems that might arise. I had survived my SCA and I now had medication to control my condition. We were dealing with it as a family.

GENETICS

Cardiomyopathy is most often inherited and is the most common form of genetic heart disease. Understanding genetics can be difficult and the process of identifying the genes can take a long time.

As I mentioned, my blood was taken whilst in hospital as my consultant recommended I had genetic testing to find out if I had the affected gene.

I received confirmation from the genetics team in July that my case had been discussed and an offer of genetic testing and counselling should be made. A telephone interview was scheduled. During the interview, they asked for information including my family history and a family tree as far back as my grandparents.

This was not an easy task; all my grandparents are deceased. I never met one of my grandfathers, as he died when my mum was 16; my other grandfather died in 1977 and both my grandmothers died in 1990. Fortunately, I do have information about their deaths, and death certificates for three of them, but I know not everyone has access to so much information. Both my parents are also deceased, so information was obtained from my aunt and through documentation.

My father was a participant of nuclear testing on Christmas Island as part of Operation Dominic in 1962. A study in 2007 by the New Zealand Nuclear Test Veterans Association and Dr Al Rowland showed that the DNA of the participants of nuclear testing showed abnormal translocations. Could the testing have affected my father? Did he have the gene, but we never knew? He died in 1994 and was never tested for the gene or for cardiomyopathy.

There are still so many questions relating to our family history: the early deaths of my father and brother, my sister's heart attack... Whilst we wait for the answers, at least we know that, at the present time, neither my sister or my son are showing any signs of cardiomyopathy.

Genetic testing advances every day. New techniques are being developed that will help us understand our conditions and how our genetic makeup may be passed on to future generations. Research is being undertaken constantly with funding being made available to understand the condition.

Helping as much as possible with this, answering surveys, being available if asked to undertake studies is something I am keen to do. Helping others through the process, helping researchers and educating people will save lives.

HELPING RAISE AWARENESS

As a family, we wanted to help raise awareness of SCA, cardiomyopathy, CPR and defibrillators as much as possible, in any way possible.

Mel has already run a half marathon for Cardiomyopathy UK, football colleagues walked 100K and I gave a talk at the legacy event for Wales Air Ambulance;. Mel has also run 5 miles to raise funds for a local defibrillator.

This is only the start of what we want to achieve. This book will hopefully help families who have experienced an SCA. I have been given an extension to my life. Some people call it a re-birthday or a second chance. I like to call it an extension.

Before my SCA and diagnosis, I was not aware of cardiomyopathy, but I had heard extremely sad stories about people dying of SCAs on the news, some of them extremely young.

There is no doubt that CPR and defibrillators save lives. I welcomed the news that defibrillators will be installed in all English schools. CPR should be taught to everyone. You may never need to use it but being able to perform it may save someone.

Defibrillators should be installed in as many places as possible and people made aware of how to locate one. The British Heart Foundation has created a website called The Circuit, which allows anyone to register their defibrillator at www.thecircuit.uk. You can search a database of registered defibrillators by visiting www.defibfinder.uk.

I would encourage you to enter your postcode or any location you might be visiting for an event and check to see where the defibrillators are. Quick access to a defibrillator really makes a difference. I am living proof of that.

Obviously, as a family we are now engaged with organisations and support groups that helped me, but there is no reason why you cannot support organisations such as your local air ambulance; you never know when you may require their services. Most now run a lottery and this is the easiest way to help them.

The Wales Air Ambulance has to raise £6 million a year to keep operating. That is a massive amount of money and any support they receive is greatly appreciated.

I have registered to become a volunteer for Wales Air Ambulance, helping wherever possible, utilising my current free time to give something back to the charity, who have been so supportive during difficult times.

If we can all help organisations like the ones mentioned above, in whatever way, however small, it will help them make a difference to people's lives. If you can, join their lottery schemes, volunteer or fundraise for them.

MAKING A WILL

When you are younger, making a will is something that never enters your mind. When you buy your first home, you may take out life insurance and then make a will, but it is something that never seems important.

I had a will, but it was out of date. I had got married and moved house since the last one, and it no longer reflected my wishes. And when I attended the legacy event for Wales Air Ambulance and listened to a presentation about the implications of inheritance tax, I was shocked when Sabrina said it was 40% in the UK; I thought she must have said 14%! The reality is the inheritance rules in the UK are very complex, and an allocation is made for certain amounts of money, but the UK Government takes 40% on anything above that figure.

Following that event, we arranged an appointment to discuss our wills with Sabrina. Mel did not have one at all and the shock of my SCA had made us both think about the future. Hopefully, I will be around for many years to come, but, after the SCA scare, it was something that needed urgent attention.

The process was easy. We discussed our finances, our investments and property and Sabrina drew up the wills. We also discussed Power of Attorney for if anything was to happen to me or they needed to turn off my ICD for any reason.

Death is not a nice subject to discuss at any time, but if you have children, insurance, a mortgage or possessions you want to give to specific people, you should make a will.

Many of us have children or partners who we want to provide for after we are gone. Wills give specific instructions of our wishes. Without a will, it can lead to family arguments, the loss of income through inheritance tax and other issues.

Knowing where your insurance policies and will are stored is something you should get in order now. If you have a safe in your house, or a filing cabinet or area where you store important documents such as passports etc., make sure your executor knows where it is and, if there is a key code, what it is. Having to break into a safe where important documents are kept because only you knew the combination is not something your loved ones want to do after you are gone.

Many people do not plan for their death. It is not the nicest of subjects to discuss with your loved ones, especially at an early age. But if you can, make a will at the very least. Ask your favourite charity for a pack – many will-making packs can be obtained for free. Do your research and seek legal advice before it is too late.

For every family that has experienced an SCA, you

will understand that life changes in an instant. The entire family is affected and is left to pick up the pieces in very distressing circumstances. Having paperwork in an easy-to-access place with everything in order will help a lot.

WORK

Before my SCA, I was working as a data protection officer for ICARIS Sentinel Ltd, a company I set up many years before. I also own ICARIS Ltd, which provides software solutions to not-for-profit organisations across the world.

My role involved processing subject access requests, advising clients on all aspects of data protection (including audits of sites) and responding to data breaches. Under UK Data Protection laws, you have 72 hours from the breach point to fully investigate and then decide to report to the Information Commissioner's Office (the governing body). This 72 hours includes bank holidays and weekends, so a serious data breach can involve a lot of meetings, visits to the location of the breach and intense work, something I could no longer do because of my health and my driving ban.

Obviously, we had bills to pay; everyone has bills that need to be paid: rent, mortgage and utilities as well as food. During the initial few weeks following my cardiac arrest, the bills were not important. Coming through my ordeal, looking after my health and ensuring I would recover from my SCA was top priority. For those who are not so lucky, who have lost a loved one to an SCA, the grief is huge. We as a family lost my father and brother to heart attacks and my mother never recovered.

However, as time passes, the subject of money and how to cope with life-changing events financially comes to mind. Many people do not have savings; they rely on monthly income to pay bills and keep a roof over their head. As I said before, we had life insurance with critical illness and income protection, but not everyone has such provision. We also had to remember that the payments would take months to sort out and there was a 13-week deferment period for income protection insurance.

For the first three months of my recovery we suspended work contracts and I was paid Statutory Sick Pay, which did not cover the mortgage payments. We relied on savings to ensure that the basic bills were paid.

After the initial three months, I still did not feel able to return to work in my current role and my doctor signed me off work for another three months to ensure my body recovered sufficiently. It was at this point that I decided I would never return to my role in its current form; I could not possibly perform the emergency part of a contract that was needed.

So, what to do? As the owner of ICARIS, I was extremely lucky to have a dedicated workforce who would ensure the business continued to operate under the instruction of the Managing Director, who has been handling the day-to-day running of the business for many years.

We discussed the contract with the client, and we decided to cancel it. This was a big decision to make. The contract paid well and it would be a big loss to my income and that of the business, but it was not fair on the client or myself – and my health had to come first. We continued other contracts with the client, but the data protection services were terminated and we decided to shut down ICARIS Sentinel and concentrate on ICARIS.

I understand how difficult it must be for anyone to make such decisions, whether they are employed or self-employed. Discussing the situation with employers or clients can be very difficult, especially if it is the main source of income for the family.

As you'll have already read, at the time of writing this book I have decided I will not be returning to IT at all. I have finished my MBA and am awaiting the results, and I am going to retrain as a counsellor and help others as much as possible. It will take three years to complete and will be a new chapter in my life.

I have always helped others. Through our Community Interest Company LABRATS, we help nuclear veteran communities across the world, and I have always been interested in counselling, so it was the obvious choice. Alongside my training via college and online courses, I'll also be volunteering for various organisations.

This change in direction is possible for me, but may not be possible for everyone. You may love your job and want to return to it, or you may be forced to do so for financial reasons. Then again, returning to work may not be an option for some, especially those who are self-employed.

From my experience, it takes time. We all have different experiences and diagnosis can be difficult to come to terms with but remain strong and continue the path to recovery. Change in our lives can be for the good, even forced change.

For me, it was a realisation that the hours I had put in, the late nights and the stress had not really been worth it and my work-life balance had to change.

The thought of leaving behind Mel, Joseph, my family and friends was a lot to handle. My life had changed forever: I had been granted an extension to my life, as such, and I needed to take it and enjoy it as much as possible.

Time is a good healer. If you are returning to work, make sure you are fit and well enough, and don't be afraid to ask for help. Many employers will be sympathetic to your situation and will help as much as possible.

DAY TO DAY

At the beginning of my journey we took one day at a time, understanding what had caused my SCA and what my treatment was going to be, receiving scan results, and undergoing tests. You live on a day-to-day basis and your whole world revolves around the hospital. When you leave hospital, initially you still work daily, getting used to medication and recovering from surgery.

Feeling battered and bruised and extremely tired after surgery and feeling the effects of new medication is hard. One day you are OK and have no issues, the next you feel as if you have been run over by a bus.

Your whole world has been turned upside down, mentally, and physically you are exhausted. You have been told there is a long road to recovery, and you may have been diagnosed with underlying problems such as cardiomyopathy (as I was).

It was hard, and life had changed, but I had to be thankful that I was still alive. My father and brother were not so lucky, and I had witnessed the impact it had on my mother, losing her husband and oldest son in the space of 18 months.

It is very easy to become depressed. My

cardiologist told me not to lift anything heavy, or over my head, with my left arm for six weeks because of my ICD. Simple things like putting on a hoodie were difficult. My wife came up with the idea of cutting the back of a few old T-shirts so I didn't have to lift my arm, which worked brilliantly. But six weeks is a long time to be relying on others.

Waiting for the bruising to subside, the pain from broken ribs and the fatigue were all new experiences and I found the first few weeks extremely hard. When you are an active person, being told to sit in bed and rest is difficult. Netflix became my main companion!

The fatigue was the worst. Falling asleep in a chair, constant yawning, feeling tired and often not being awake for more than a few hours a day.

As time went by, the scar above my ICD healed, I was able to shower, and the bruises started to subside. My ribs were still extremely painful, but I was more mobile and able to get up and walk a short distance. As most people do, I always did too much, and I would feel the pain and the tiredness for days to come when I overdid it. Some of this was the side effects of my medicine, but it was also my body dealing with the trauma it had been through.

At my six-week check I was given the all clear to lift my left arm and to start more walking and doing more activities. It was a great lift to my spirits. I knew I would never be the same, but I wanted to continue to be as active as I could. I attended Joseph's football matches and watched the training sessions for the walking football. But I felt sorry for Mel, who was now my carer and chauffeur!

My days were the same. Get up, take medicine, make a few phone calls regarding our not-for-profit, talk to the MD of ICARIS, Facetime family, have food, fall asleep, shower and go to bed. Some days felt like Groundhog Day and as time passed it became extremely frustrating not being able to drive.

My ICD was giving me pain in my left shoulder if I typed too much, so I tried to limit my time at the computer, but it was difficult as the campaign for the nuclear veterans was gathering pace and needed my attention.

Five months later, the pain has eased. There are still good days and bad days and I am still tired most of the time, but it is getting easier. My ICD hasn't fired, and it has now become part of me. I am desperate to get back to playing walking football again, but I am waiting until the full six months to make sure I am fit enough to play.

My life is not the same and I do not think it will ever be. I am now a different person. My life has been changed forever, but I must remember that I have a second chance, an extension to my life, which my brother and father never had. I am a 1 in 10 survivor.

LIVING DIFFERENTLY

Whilst browsing the online forums, I came across a post entitled *Living Differently*. It was a discussion about not giving in to the SCA and the diagnosis, but embracing it, learning from it and using it as a stepping stone to move forward and enjoy life.

This is easier said than done. Your mind will suddenly throw in a memory or the realisation that you were dead, could easily have not survived and could easily have been brain damaged. It can come at any moment: during a TV programme or an advert, when reading a story on an online forum or just randomly popping into your head.

Living differently is such a good term for what I am doing. I am living, still here and working towards recovery, just in a different way.

Jobs that I used to do are still out of my reach, such as cutting the grass, clearing gutters etc. I must believe that the situation will not be forever, and I will return, but it will take time.

My condition can be controlled with medication, hopefully, and with the stents. My artery is clear and I am in a better place, knowing my condition and having the backup of an ICD.

I am determined not to sit on my backside and feel sorry for myself. There are people whose loved ones don't make it and others who have been left with terrible brain damage. Every day, I wake up and think how lucky I am. I get to see my son grow up; I get to experience life and enjoy my time.

It is different, there is no doubt about it. Medicines, doctors' visits, hospital appointments, being careful, making sure I have enough medication, waking up and feeling tired even after a good night's sleep are all new experiences.

My mind wanders sometimes, or I get words wrong in a sentence, which makes us all laugh. I have trouble remembering things, but it does come to me eventually. I know my HCM will never be cured and I have this condition for the rest of my life, but at least I know about it and can deal with it.

I know that without the medical attention, being in the right place with a defibrillator and the air ambulance, I would be dead. I *was* effectively dead. Mentally, this is something that is difficult to come to terms with. I have so much still to do for nuclear veterans and their families and so much more life to live – and that could all have ended on 3rd April 2022.

Everyone I meet says, "You look well," and sometimes I do feel well, but other times I am not, I'm exhausted or having a bad day. I look at the situation I am in and say to myself that it is a miracle I survived and I must use the time wisely and not get stressed by situations; it is not worth it. I am no longer going to work myself into an early grave. My father and brother were robbed of the major part of their lives, and it is not going to happen to me.

Some things are beyond our control – side effects of medicine, for instance – and we have to live with it, get through it and continue to smile. Using humour is a great way to do this: funny T-shirts or laughing about words that come out at the wrong times all helps. Just smiling, knowing you survived and have been given a second chance helps.

For some, their lives are forever affected. Losing a loved one is extremely difficult, and life-changing injuries can put a strain on any family, but as my gran would say, you have to take the bumps in the road of life. Some are small and others large enough to impact you and damage you, but keep going and keep smiling through it all.

We are all time limited; we never know when our lives will end, so enjoy it and keep going.

ADVICE

I wanted to finish this book with some links to online support groups and other websites that I have found to be extremely helpful. I also wanted to summarise my journey so far. It is not yet complete, but I hope it will help.

It has been extremely difficult for me and my family and there is no doubt my SCA has changed all our lives forever. I am so lucky to have survived. So many others are not so lucky, and the grief felt by their families is something no one should have to experience.

It is a shock for anyone who experiences an SCA or diagnosis of a heart condition that will affect them for the rest of their life. Anyone who has been present during an SCA, performed CPR or has been affected will understand how life-changing the experience is.

When I heard the 1 in 10 statistic, it really hit me hard, knowing that if I had been in a different place, on my own or even driving the car, I would not be writing this. It takes time to come to terms with what has happened. For survivors, taking time to recuperate and heal is important. For partners, family and friends, it is also difficult to come to terms with the change in lifestyle. It's also difficult for those who have performed CPR, especially when the person does not survive. It can be a very distressing event and one that is hard to forget.

For those who experience an SCA, I would advise you to find help, whether through your consultant, doctor, a therapist, not-for-profit organisations or online support groups. Understanding the condition and how to cope with it really helped us. Just ensure any information you find online is from a reputable source; there is too much misinformation out there that could upset you and your family.

Take your time, and seek help and guidance from professionals and others who have experienced the same issues. Join online support groups and participate in the group sessions. It really does help.

Please remember that whatever has happened to you or a loved one is a traumatic incident and it will always be there in your past; memories will come back at random moments. There will be good and bad days, but you are not alone. There are lots of people who can help you.

I read a social media post about a six-year-old boy who asked about his pet dog, who had died, and his father told him he was now with the boy's grandfather, who had also recently died. The father had recently recovered from an SCA and the boy asked him why he hadn't joined them when he died but had been given another chance. It's a difficult question to answer for us all, but especially for a child. The father could only say that he still had work to do and he needed to be there for his son so he was not left alone, not just yet.

The question of why I survived is always in my mind. Why was I at that specific location when I had my SCA, why were there people there who understood CPR, why was a defibrillator available? The list goes on. The questions still play in my head, and I think they will for many years to come, perhaps forever.

I am still on my journey to recovery. I know the path I am travelling is a new one, and it's one that was unexpected, but one I will embrace and enjoy taking. I hope that however far you are along your new path, you stay safe and well and enjoy your second chance at life.

For those who have lost loved ones, I am truly sorry for your loss. Grief is a terrible thing to experience and it never leaves us. I still mourn the death of my family members, 28 years on. Time helps, and keeping the memories alive helps. Writing this book has helped me and I hope that it can help you too.

Over the months, I have found many online support groups and products that can help. Here are a few of them.

Sudden Cardiac Arrest UK
www.suddencardiacarrestuk.org

This organisation is for anyone affected by a sudden cardiac arrest, whether you are a survivor, rescuer, partner, family member or an interested medical professional.

- info@suddencardiacarrestuk.org
- www.twitter.com/WeAreSCAUK
- facebook.com/SuddenCardiacArrestUK
- facebook.com/groups/SuddenCardiacArrestUK (Facebook group: for social interaction, chat, stories, questions and advice)

They also published a book called *Life After Cardiac Arrest* by Paul Swindell, which is an excellent read.

Cardiomyopathy UK
www.cardiomyopathy.org

Cardiomyopathy UK is the UK's specialist national charity for people affected by cardiomyopathy, a condition that affects the heart muscle. Their vision is that everyone affected by cardiomyopathy should live a long and fulfilling life.

- www.facebook.com/cardiomyopathyuk
- www.twitter.com/cardiomyopathy
- www.instagram.com/cardiomyopathyuk/

Chain of Survival

www.facebook.com/groups/643122902711790

This is a group for those in the UK (or UK expats) who have been involved in or are interested in the 'Chain of Survival' i.e. providing emergency care when loss of life is imminent, such as during cardiac arrest when CPR or AED shocks are given. This group has grown out of the Sudden Cardiac Arrest UK group, which supports those affected by that condition. There is an overlap in the two groups in that many family members become part of a survivor's chain of survival, but there are other members of this group for whom SCA UK may not be appropriate.

British Heart Foundation

www.bhf.org.uk

BHF funds around £100 million of research each year into all heart and circulatory diseases and the things that cause them. Heart diseases, stroke, vascular dementia and diabetes are all connected, and they're all under British Heart Foundation's microscope.

- www.facebook.com/bhf
- www.twitter.com/TheBHF

Defib Finder UK

www.defibfinder.uk

This site provides up to date information on

defibrillator locations across the UK, using data from The Circuit, the national defibrillator network. Enter your location to find the nearest defibrillators to you. Then simply click on the defibrillator icons for further information, such as availability, access information and directions.

ICD Support UK
www.facebook.com/groups/787996791252240

Friendly group for discussion, advice, help and support for people with an ICD or who have relatives/friends etc with an ICD.

Sudden Arrhythmic Death UK
www.sadsuk.org.uk

The cardiac charity SADS UK aims to save lives, providing information, funding research and medical equipment to prevent premature sudden cardiac death. Working in the areas of research, prevention and emergency care, lives have been saved as a direct result of the work of SADS UK. They hold the Annual National Lifesaver Awards to honour people who have saved lives in the community using CPR and the defibrillator.

SADS UK highlights the fact that young people and even children can be affected by potentially fatal cardiac conditions. SADS UK is one of the founder members of SADS International, a worldwide

network of SADS organisations led by people who have been affected personally by SADS, or work closely with those who have.
- www.twitter.com/SADSUK
- www.facebook.com/groups/6866652676/

Vital Beat

www.vitalbeat.com

Getting a life-saving device implanted has a really big impact on your life. Though it is meant to keep you healthy and well, it does come with a cost, including pain, discomfort, constant worrying and countless restrictions in your life regarding sports, vacation and leisure activities.

Vital Beat comfort and protection helps you and your loved ones make the most of life again by protecting your device during your favourite sports and activities, making it comfortable to use a seatbelt, backpack and safety harness, and letting you enjoy your leisure time and hobbies without worries.

Insurance Companies

I am yet to travel overseas, but I am reassured by the community that there are companies who will insure people after an SCA as well as those with an ICD and cardiomyopathy. This is of great importance to me, as not being able to travel abroad to see relatives would be a massive blow.

- Staysure: www.staysure.co.uk
- All Clear: www.allcleartravel.co.uk

Wales Air Ambulance
www.walesairambulance.com

'Everyone in Wales deserves fast critical care whenever and wherever they are.'

Glasgow Coma Scale
www.glasgowcomascale.org

ADDENDUM

As this book goes to print, I wanted to provide an update on my situation. On 15th October 2022, I received my driving licence back from DVLA. I had sent the application in early, and Professor Yousef filled in the forms and sent them back immediately. I am extremely grateful to him for taking the time to clear me to drive again. The freedom that comes with being able to drive is fantastic. For anyone reading this who is waiting for their licence, I sympathise with you and hope you receive it soon. I encourage you to contact DVLA as they were very efficient and helpful with me when I contacted the medical team.

I have also returned to walking football training, taking part in a few sessions to try and increase my fitness. I am extremely grateful to the team at Carmarthen Town who have welcomed me back and looked after my family, especially Joseph who has been training with them regularly.

I have been signed off work until 3rd January 2023 and I am still evaluating my options regarding returning to work. My doctor has discussed the possibility of taking medical retirement and I am currently looking at all the options available to me and how it will affect our lives and our income. Looking at benefits, pensions and other income protection plans to ensure I can provide for the family is a difficult task.

I am changing medication from Ramipril, as it is giving me a cough and a very dry throat. I am being switched to Losartan, hopefully with no side effects.

On Friday 14th October 2022, I attended the Wales Air Ambulance Gala Dinner, where a video I made for the event was shown. I met Sian Andrews, who suffered a cardiac arrest the day after me and spent 78 days in ICU. She was incredible, and we will be meeting up for coffee and a chat. Receiving a standing ovation from the audience was very humbling and brought waves of emotion for us both. The team are incredible, the service they provide is amazing and their dedication to the cause is fantastic.

I have now qualified for Employment Support Allowance (ESA) as my statutory sick pay has ran out, this will help us to ensure that we continue to be financially stable.

Life is still difficult, day to day, mentally and physically, but it is still only eight months since my SCA, and I know it will take time. I take every positive step as a win and every step backwards as just another hurdle to overcome. Waking up every day is a gift for us all.

I am now officially volunteering for the Wales Air Ambulance, giving talks about their service and how it saved my life. This will allow me to give something back to the service.

One of my colleagues told me that I survived my SCA because I still had work to do, that there was unfinished business for me to attend to. In November, as part of LABRATS, we marched on 10 Downing Street, laid wreaths at the Cenotaph and held a small rally at the Ministry of Defence building.

(Details of the campaign can be found at www.labrats.international/lookmeintheeye).

This day really took its toll on me. It was an extremely long day, but worth it to protest at the lack of a medal award from the UK Government to the nuclear veterans.

The Office for Veterans' Affairs had agreed to a commemorative event at the National Memorial Arboretum (NMA) on 21st November to remember the veterans and their service, including those who did not make it this far and had sadly passed away.

I was determined to attend and made plans with my sister to drive to her house in Cheltenham and then stay the night and go on to the NMA at Alrewas, Staffordshire. Despite the cold and very wet weather, we set off and I was informed just before the ceremony that we had achieved our goal. The UK Government was finally going to recognise the participants of the testing programme with a medal. It was fantastic news and something that I had been campaigning for since 2017.

So perhaps that person was right, I did have

unfinished business, and I was glad I was present when the Prime Minister, Rishi Sunak, announced the award.

We are now in December and the medication change has taken some getting used to. It has made me more tired, but I am determined to ensure that the medal is crafted and awarded at a special ceremony for the veterans and that I will be able to attend.

It was a very special day for my sister and me. We finally had my father's legacy honoured by the UK Government. It was a day I never thought I would see – and a day I almost didn't see.

The air ambulances at the scene

The Wales Air Ambulance crew who saved my life

Joseph and me in the air ambulance

With the team at Caldicot Leisure Centre

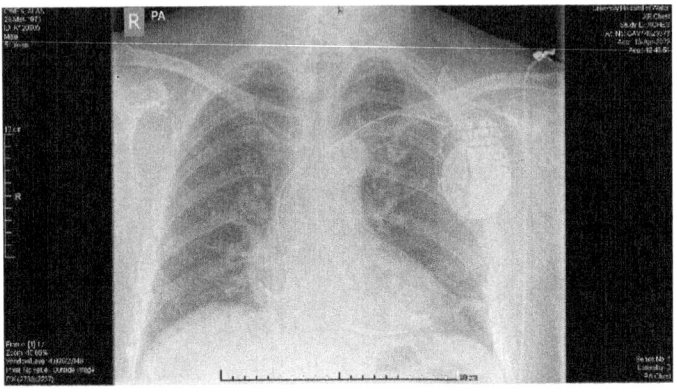

Top: X-ray of my ICD implant

Bottom: Ruby and me at the Wales Air Ambulance gala dinner

Printed in Great Britain
by Amazon